Joseph ⟨ S0-BJM-103 ⟩er

Pocket Color Atlas of Dermatology

American Edition Translated and Revised by
Herbert Goldschmidt
302 Figures in Color

1975
Year Book Medical Publishers, Inc.
Georg Thieme Publishers Stuttgart

J. KIMMIG, M. D., Professor of Dermatology, Chief of the Department and Dispensary, University Hospital, Hamburg

M. JÄNNER, M. D., Professor of Dermatology, Department of Dermatology and Dispensary, University Hospital, Hamburg

H. GOLDSCHMIDT, M. D., F.A.C.P., Associate Clinical Professor of Dermatology, University of Pennsylvania Medical School, Philadelphia, Pennsylvania

Distributed in Continental North, South and Central America, Hawaii, Puerto Rico, and The Philippines by Year Book Medical Publishers, Inc.

Year Book Medical Publishers, Inc. 1975

ISBN 0-8151-5050-4
Library of Congress Catalog Card Number 74-21026

Preface to the English Edition

"One good picture is worth a thousand words", this saying applies to dermatologic teaching more than to any other specialty training. Of all the organ systems the skin is obviously the one most suited to photographic reproduction. Significant advances in the technology of color photography and color printing processes have made it possible to produce illustrations extraordinarily faithful to the living state.

This pocket edition of our color atlas presents 302 selected color illustrations of common skin diseases and provides excellent visual clues to less common cutaneous disorders. Some skin diseases which are encountered by every physician almost daily are depicted in several illustrations to demonstrate nuances of diagnostic significance.

The English edition of this work was carefully revised and adapted to include recent advances in clinical dermatology and newer diagnostic terms and concepts. Each illustration carries a brief legend emphasizing important diagnostic details. Eighty pages of text provide the reader with short reviews of all major cutaneous disorders and venereal diseases. To the dermatologic novice the pocket color atlas serves as a very useful visual complement to more detailed textbooks; to the more experienced it offers a refresher course in dermatologic differential diagnosis with color reproductions of excellent quality at a reasonable cost.

Philadelphia, November 1974   HERBERT GOLDSCHMIDT

Extract from preface to the German Edition

Daily contact with medical students and young residents has taught us that even those who have a solid theoretical basis in dermatology may find themselves deficient in visual diagnostic skills when confronted with dermatological patients. By showing the morphology of cutaneous and venereal disorders in color photographs, we hope to help our young colleagues overcome this discrepancy and to aid established dermatologists in keeping their diagnostic skills on a high level.

Undoubtedly the best way to learn about dermatoses is by direct and systematic observation. Clinical presentations are, however, not always feasible or available. We believe that color photographs, while far from being a complete substitute, can help the student organize basic visual concepts in this specialty. The disorders shown here are predominantly prototypes which may occur in numerous variations. In this pocket edition of the Color Atlas of Dermatology we have attempted to tie together for our student readers theoretical knowledge derived from lectures, information gleaned from textbooks and journals, and visual impressions gained in clinical demonstrations.

Hamburg, September 1973

JOSEPH KIMMIG   MICHAEL JÄNNER

Table of Contents

Macular Eruptions

Erythematous macular eruptions

Erythema, the most common reaction of the skin, is due to dilatation of the capillaries (hyperemia). The affected skin blanches momentarily on diascopic examination with a glass slide, but the redness reappears as soon as the pressure is relieved. A variety of causes may be responsible for active (inflammatory) or passive (stasis) hyperemia.

Erythema may be localized or widespread, ranging from minute macules to involvement of the entire body surface, as in erythrodermas. According to their configuration, the patches are classified as annular, gyrate, circinate, or serpiginous erythemas. Macules covering the entire integument in regular distribution are often called exanthemata (Figs. 1—3).

When active hyperemia is followed by edema, extravasation, and infiltration, the erythema may assume a polymorphous appearance of urticarial, vesicular, hemorrhagic, or papular character.

Erythema Infectiosum Variabile
(Margarine Disease)

An epidemic erythematous eruption involving thousands of patients was observed in Germany and Holland in 1958 and 1959. The exanthema appeared on the proximal parts of the extremities and sometimes on the face, usually without prodromal manifestations, and spread rapidly over the entire integument (Fig. 4). It was accompanied by severe itching and, in rare cases, by elevated temperatures. A wide variety of eruptions was seen, particularly erythema multiforme-like lesions, and morbilliform and papular eruptions. Vesicular and hemorrhagic changes were observed less frequently. On the fourth or fifth day after its onset, the exanthema began to regress, and the itching subsided.

Although a viral etiology could not be ruled out, many authors believe that this protean eruption was caused by a new emulsifier used in the production of margarine in those countries.

Erythema Chronicum Migrans (Lipschütz - Afzelius)

This disease usually starts with red macules, which develop into ringed erythematous lesions with light red, only slightly raised migrating margins and pale or livid centers (Fig. 5). In some cases the eruption seems to follow inset bites, especially tick bites. Viruses or toxins contained in tick saliva have been discussed as etiologic agents. This disorder is extremely rare on the American continent.

Erythema Multiforme (von Hebra)

The classic, idiopathic erythema multiforme is characterized by symmetrical, bright bluish red to dark purple, slightly infiltrated, round macules with a tendency to spread peripherally. These lesions are found on the dorsal aspects of hands, fingers, feet, and toes, and on the adjacent areas of the extremities. They may or may not be accompanied by systemic symptoms. In the initial stage, the central portion of the lesions usually shows a bluish-gray discoloration, which is intensified during the next few days; simultaneously, a central depression develops. As a rule, the polymorphous lesions subside completely after a few more days.

In other cases, the disorder may manifest itself in concentric rings (target or iris lesions) (Fig. 6) or in peculiar circinate lesions with peripheral rings and central disks showing a lighter color than the midzone. Other variants are characterized by large blisters (bullous erythema multiforme), which may contain a hemorrhagic exsudate.

In the form of large blisters, the disease may also affect the buccal mucosa, sometimes in combination with the cutaneous changes described above. In some cases, especially in male patients, the genitals may become involved. In its severe, sometimes fatal generalized form, the disease is often classified as Stevens-Johnson syndrome. It mostly affects children and young adults, and starts with high fever, malaise and severe stomatitis, conjunctivitis, urethritis, and balanitis, followed later by the typical skin lesions of erythema multiforme (Fig. 7).

Despite its characteristic morphology, erythema multiforme is not an etiologic entity but a reaction pattern.

The *idiopathic form* of the disease is probably of viral etiology. Herpes simplex labialis frequently precedes the onset of this type, which often has a seasonal incidence (spring or fall).

Symptomatic forms, closely resembling the idiopathic type in their morphology, may be due to internal medication (salicylates, sulfonamides, hydantoin derivatives, phenacetin, barbiturates, iodides, bromides) or may follow systemic diseases (bacterial or viral infections, allergic disorders, malignancies). The symptomatic form of erythema multiforme seldom involves the buccal mucosa; typical iris lesions are rare.

Erythema Nodosum (von Hebra)

This syndrome is characterized by successive crops of symmetrical, bright red, tender nodules with smooth surface, varying in size from 1 to 5 cm., and occasionally coalescing to form large indurations on the lower extremities (Fig. 8). Vascular damage may lead to extravasation of blood and, due to degradation of hemoglobin, to greenish or bluish-yellow purpuric discolorations (contusiform type of erythema nodosum). Ulceration is extremely rare. Predilection sites are the anterior surfaces of the lower legs, less often those of the thighs. At times, the extensor surfaces of the arms may be affected. The disease is self-limited and occurs chiefly in young adults. Recurrent and seasonal forms are not rare. The attacks are often associated with mild constitutional symptoms such as malaise, fever, and pains in muscles and joints.

Symptomatic forms include nodular cutaneous reactions associated with infectious diseases, particularly streptococcal infections (scarlet fever, rheumatic fever), fungal infections (coccidioidomycosis), tuberculosis (in children), leprosy, chicken pox, lymphogranuloma venereum, and syphilis. The erythema nodosum reaction pattern can also be elicited by drugs (iodides, bromides, sulfonamides, penicillin). It also can bee sen in sarcoidosis.

Toxic Epidermal Necrolysis (Lyell)

This grave, often fatal syndrome has an acute onset with localized or disseminated erythematous lesions. Advanced stages are characterized by large flaccid blisters. The epidermis sloughs off in large sheets, as in a widespread scalding burn, leaving a moist, dark red, raw dermal surface. The disease is associated with fever and severe systemic manifestations; the mucous membranes are often involved (Fig. 9). In some cases the disorder is caused by allergic or toxic drug reactions (e.g., to sulfonamides, hydantoin, antipyrine); other cases are associated with infections, especially with phage-type 71 staphylococci.

Erythema Annulare Centrifugum (Darier)

This syndrome has an abrupt onset but usually runs a chronic, often recurrent course; its cause is unknown. An initial erythema develops into a large wheal, which rapidly grows eccentrically with a raised urticarial border, while the central portion returns to the level of the surrounding normal skin, leaving a yellowish or faintly pigmented, slightly scaling surface. Polycyclic and gyrate configurations are frequently seen (Fig. 10). In the course of several weeks, new lesions replace the old ones. The disease predominantly affects adults, involving primarily the trunk and the proximal portions of the extremities. Similar eruptions have been described as autoimmune reactions, dermatophytids (trichophytin test), and in association with rheumatoid arthritis and internal malignant tumors.

Purpura

Morphologically, three main varieties of purpura are described. Petechiae are superficial hemorrhagic macules that are round, 1 to 5 mm. in diameter, and sharply outlined. Ecchymoses are slightly deeper and more extensive round or irregular extravasations. Hematomas are large, deep bluish, rounded, poorly outlined fluctuant collections of extravasated blood.

Cutaneous hemorrhages are not a disease entity. Unlike erythematous eruptions, extravasations of blood (hemosiderin) into the skin cannot be blanched by diascopy (firm pressure with a glass slide). Exanthematous patterns of blood extravasations into the skin are described clinically as *purpura*. Some forms of purpura are entirely benign, where as others may signify extremely serious diseases. Clinical and laboratory tests permit differentiation of: (1) purpura with coagulation defects, (2) purpura with thrombocytic defects (thrombocytopenia, thrombasthenia), and (3) purpura with vascular damage (damage to the capillary endothelium due to hypoxemia, allergic reactions, or vitamin deficiency).

Idiopathic Thrombocytopenic Purpura (Werlhof)

Petechiae or ecchymoses, usually of a pronounced purple or bluish color, are characteristic of this disorder (Fig. 11). Diagnosis is based on blood tests, an episodic course, hemorrhages into the mucous membranes, internal hemorrhages, higher incidence in young females than in males, splenomegaly, and positive Rumpel-Leede sign. The acute allergic form often follows infections, shows massive purpuric lesions, and is usually self-limited. The chronic form has a gradual onset and a long history of easy bruising and bleeding of mucous membranes, frequently with gestrointestinal hemorrhages; typical cutaneous purpura is less commun.

Symptomatic Thrombocytopenia

The symptomatic thrombocytopenias are of great clinical importance. Severe toxic infections (septicemia, scarlet fever, virus infections, tuberculosis), tumors with bone marrow metastases, leukemia, hypersplenism, pancytopenia, radiation damage, and drug reactions (quinine, diphenylhydantoin, sulfonamides, salicylates) are frequently associated with marked thrombocytopenia leading to cutaneous and mucosal hemorrhages.

Purpura due to vascular Damage

The common criterion of this rather heterogeneous group is vascular damage; defects in coagulation factors and platelets are less important.

The principal pathogenetic factors are vitamin C deficiency and disturbance of vitamin C utilization in the case of *scurvy*; degenerative changes of the vascular walls and surrounding connective tissue in the case of *senile purpura*; and increased hydrostatic pressure resulting in breakage of capillary walls in the case of *stasis purpura* and the pigmented purpuric eruptions of Majocchi's, Schamberg's, and Gougerot-Blum's diseases. These latter entities are probably the same disease with slightly different morphology.

Purpura Annularis Telangiectodes (Majocchi)

In this disease symmetrically arranged, pink telangiectatic punctae develop into small macular hemorrhages of reddish-brown coloration, usually on the lower legs. Ring-like configurations may occur (Fig. 12) and central atrophy may develop in extensive lesions. The disease causes no appreciable discomfort. In patients with high blood pressure, the purpuric changes are due to functional peripheral vasoconstriction and vascular damage. The incidence of the disease is highest in middle-aged males.

Progressive Pigmentary Dermatosis (Schamberg)

This syndrome, which also is more common in middle-aged men, probably represents a variant of the purpura described above. Ring formations are absent. Predominant features are poorly outlined brownish-yellow or reddish patches of varying size, with peripheral punctate petechiae; the color is described as resembling cayenne pepper (Fig. 13). Differential diagnosis includes drug eruptions.

Pigmented Purpuric Lichenoid Dermatitis (Gougerot-Blum)

The eruption usually involves the lower extremities (rarely the trunk), is often pruritic, and resembles Schamberg's disease. It is characterized by lichenoid, polygonal, flat-topped, slightly elevated purpuric papules densely grouped within brownish plaques. The papules later assume a bluish to brownish-red tinge — "embedded grains of paprika."

Schönlein's Purpura

This hemorrhagic syndrome is also known as allergic, anaphylactoid, or rheumatic purpura, or as a form of allergic vasculitis. Joint involvement is part of its symptomatology, yet its pathogenesis and pathologic anatomy are quite distinct from those of rheumatic fever. The eruption is often preceded by an infectious disease. Food and drug allergies must be ruled out.

The symmetrically arranged exanthema occurs mostly in children, showing a preference for the extensor surfaces of the legs. In severe cases, it may involve the entire integument, with the exception of popliteal and antecubital areas, palms, soles, and face. The lesions may range from discrete, pinhead- to dime-sized, pale red spots to dark red wheals or hemorrhagic vesicles (Fig. 14). Synovitis and gastrointestinal symptoms (vomiting, colicky pains, intestinal hemorrhages) may aggravate the condition. This abdominal form is also called Schönlein-Henoch *purpura* or *purpura abdominalis* Henoch.

Purpura Fulminans

This very severe, usually fatal type of purpura occurs mostly in children. The disease follows an infection and takes a rapidly progressive course resembling a Sanarelli-Shwartzman phenomenon. The preceding fulminating septicemia is often caused by Neisseria meningitidis, Streptococcus hemolyticus or Pseudomonas aeruginosa. Hemorrhages also occur in internal organs, particularly in the adrenal glands (Waterhouse-Friderichsen syndrome).

Pigmented macular eruptions

In addition to erythematous eruptions (due to dilated vessels) and purpuric lesions (due to extravasation of blood cells), macular skin lesions can also be caused by endogenous or exogenous pigments. The most important pigments causing such changes are melanin, lipofuscin, and hemosiderin.

Common variants of pigmentation due to melanin are *freckles*, *lentigines*, and *pigmented nevi*; they are only of cosmetic importance. Premalignant lesions are rare.

The *blue nevus* (nevus caeruleus) is characterized by the presence of melanocytes in the corium, as is the *Mongolian spot*. The blue nevus usually occurs singly, is sharply demarcated and not more than lentil-sized (Fig. 15). Malignant degeneration (melanosarcoma) is very rare.

Pigmentation-Polyposis Syndrome (Peutz-Jeghers)

Discrete, dark brown to black pigmented macules of irregular configuration are located about the mouth, on the oral mucosa, around the nostrils and eyes, and on the fingers and toes (Figs. 16 and 17). The disease usually occurs before the third decade and shows a high familial incidence. A thorough examination of the intestinal tract is indicated, since the skin lesions are often associated with polyposis, usually of the small intestine (abdominal pain and bleeding). Malignant degeneration of the polyps is very rare (in contrast to the potentially malignant familial polyposis of the large bowel).

Melasma (Chloasma)

Melasma presenting as *Chloasma uterinum* may occur during pregnancy (in light-exposed areas of the face). It is also seen in women who are taking progestational agents or in the presence of ovarian tumors. Perioral melasma may affect adolescent girls and young women with dysmenorrhea. Patients with hepatic disorders occasionally show periocular hyperpigmentation.

Berloque Dermatitis

Caloric stimuli may produce *melanoderma reticularis calorica* (livedo reticularis e calore). Chemical and actinic damage also may cause hyperpigmentation. The use of photosensitizers, such as eau de cologne or oil of bergamot, followed by exposure to solar radiation, may result in *berloque dermatitis* (Fig. 18).

Pellagra

Reddish-brown, sharply defined erythemas on the face, neck, and dorsa of the hands (i.e., light-exposed areas) are characteristic of *pellagra* (Fig. 19) and *pellagroids*. These disorders are due to dietary deficiency or malabsorption of nicotinic acid amide (PP-factor).

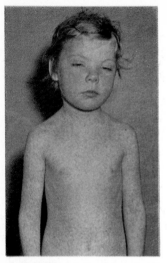 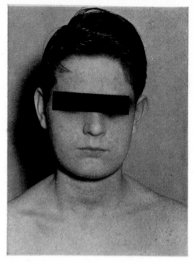

1 Measles (rubeola). Small, round or oval, reddish-brown, partially coalescing macules disseminated over the entire body surface. Photophobia.

2 German measles (rubella). Small, round or oval, pink, noncoalescing maculopapular lesions of varying size. Individual lesions are usually larger than in scarlet fever and smaller than in measles. Occipital, cervical and postauricular lymphadenopathy.

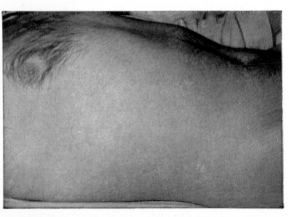

3 Scarlet fever (scarlatina). Diffuse pink-red flush of the skin with punctate (goose-flesh) papular lesions. The rash is best seen in intertriginous areas.

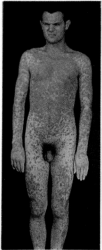
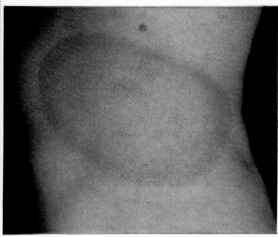

4 Erythema infectiosum variabile (infectious exanthema). Small, dusky red erythematous macules distributed over the entire integument, including scalp, palms, and soles.

5 Erythema chronicum migrans (Lipschütz). Large, oval, pale livid plaque with band-like pink raised migrating border, probably originating from a tick bite.

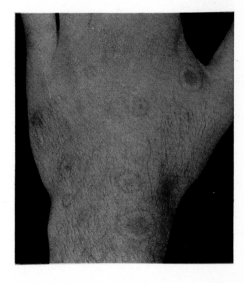

6 Erythema multiforme. Typical target lesions, formed by a new crop of annular lesions. The older central macules show a darker red color; the new peripheral lesions are pinkish.

10

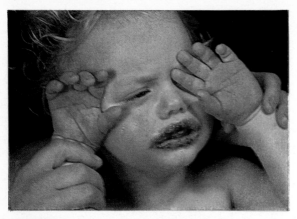

7 Stevens-Johnson syndrome. Bullous lesions, with severe involvement of mucous membranes, conjunctivitis and malaise.

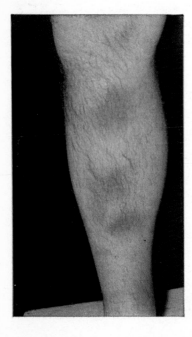

8 Erythema nodosum. Slightly raised tender, hot erythematous nodules with bruising.

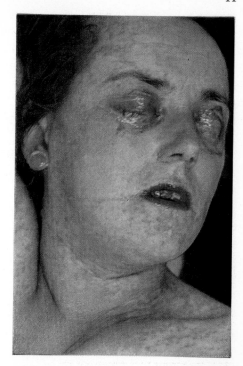

9 Toxic epidermal necrolysis (Lyell). Extensive epidermolysis resembling scalding, with severe constitutional symptoms. Oral, tracheal, and vaginal mucous membranes as well as conjunctivae are involved. Probably drug eruption.

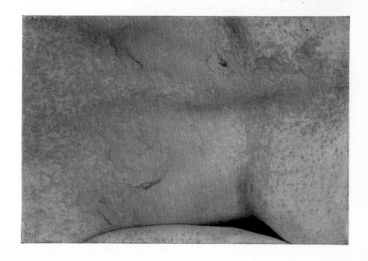

12

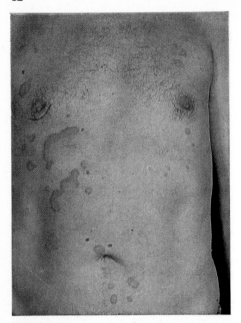

10 Erythema annulare centrifugum (Darier). Annular and serpiginous erythematous lesions with raised urticarial border on the trunk.

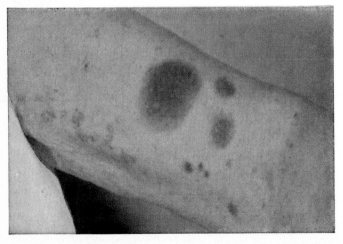

11 Idiopathic thrombocytopenic purpura (Werlhof). Extensive ecchymoses.

12 Purpura annularis telangiectodes (Majocchi). Annular and polycyclic lesions with fine petechiae. Relatively early stage, evolving from small telangiectatic purpuric macules by centrifugal extension.

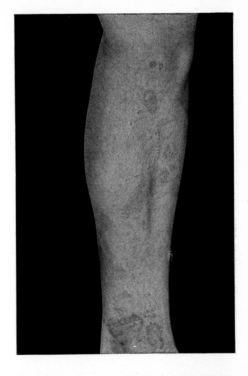

13 Progressive pigmentary dermatosis (Schamberg). Numerous petechiae on both legs.

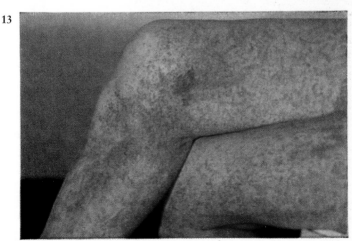

13

14

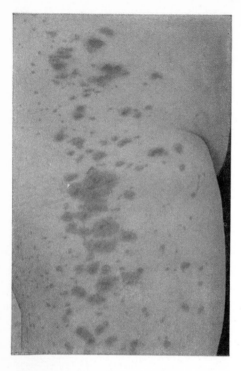

14 Schönlein's purpura.
Hemorrhages of varying size, arranged symmetrically on the lower legs and thighs, particularly on extensor surfaces. Some appear as red macules with central hemorrhagic vesicles.

15 Blue nevus (nevus caeruleus). Sharply defined, small grayish-blue nodule.

15

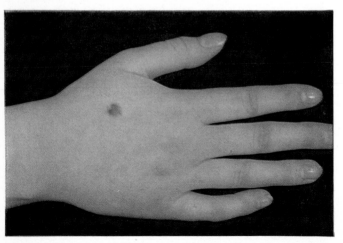

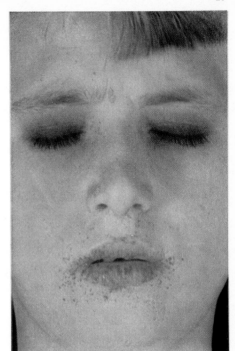

16 Pigmentation-polyposis syndrome (Peutz-Jeghers). Numerous pigmented spots on the lips and about the mouth. Oral mucosa not involved. Intestinal polyposis could not be demonstrated with certainty. One sister and one brother of the patient showed similar perioral pigmentation. The mother of this 13-year-old boy had died of malignant degeneration of intestinal polyposis.

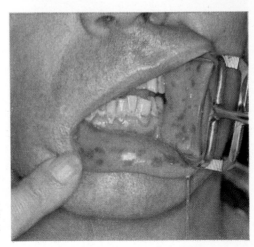

17 Pigmentation-polyposis syndrome. Pigmented spots of the oral mucosa in a young adult.

16

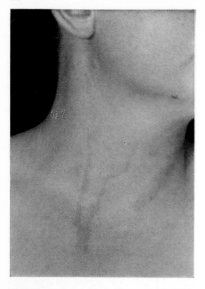

18 Berloque dermatitis. Due to application of eau de cologne to the lateral areas of the neck, followed by sun exposure.

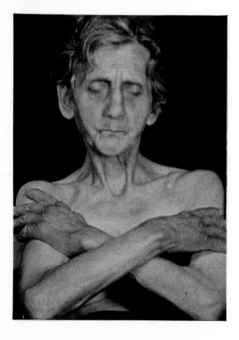

19 Pellagra. Brownish-red, sharply circumscribed erythema involving areas exposed to light, such as the face, neck, dorsa of the hands, and wrists. Fine scaling of the right hand.

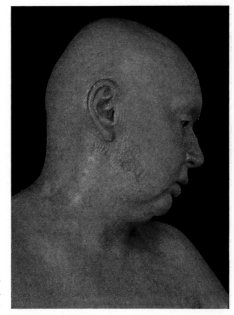

Erythrodermas

A number of dermatoses associated with erythema and scaling and involving large areas of the integument are lumped together as exfoliative dermatoses or erythrodermas; their etiology is generally unknown. Common features of primary and secondary erythrodermas are diffuse redness associated with various types of scaling, elevated temperatures, chills, and pruritus.

Primary erythrodermas are those arising in normal skin (erythroderma associated with lymphomas, Hodgkin's disease, mycosis fungoides, etc.) (Figs. 20 and 21); *secondary erythrodermas* are seen when lesions of extensive dermatoses (chronic dermatitis, neurodermatitis, seborrheic eczema, psoriasis) spread to involve the entire body surface (Fig. 22).

20 Primary erythroderma. In chronic lymphatic leukemia. Dusky red erythema and scaling (l'homme rouge).

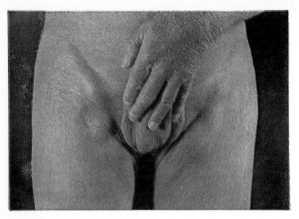

21 Primary erythroderma. Associated with lymphoma of the skin and lipomelanotic reticulosis of lymph nodes (Pautrier-Woringer).

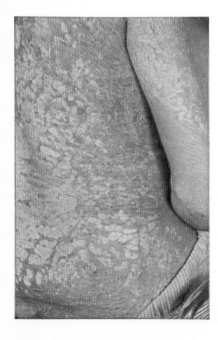

22 Secondary erythroderma. Some areas still show typical psoriatic silvery scales.

Papulosquamous Eruptions
(Erythematosquamous Dermatoses)

Psoriasis Vulgaris

The sharply circumscribed lesions of psoriasis are covered with typical dry, silvery white, shiny micaceous scales. The erythemato-papulo-squamous plaques arise from small, round, flat-topped, salmon-red papules, which are soon covered with thick white scales (Figs. 23 and 24).

Diagnostic features are the "candle phenomenon" (scrapings of psoriatic scales resemble scrapings of a candle) and Auspitz's sign (minute bleeding points corresponding to the apices of the papillae are seen upon removal of the scales and a last thin epidermal membrane). Predilection sites are the elbows and knees (mechanical irritation) as well as the scalp and lumbosacral area, but other parts of the integument may be involved as well (Fig. 25). According to site and configuration of the lesions, clinical differentiation is made between follicular, punctate, guttate, nummular, annular, gyrate, serpiginous, or confluent psoriasis. In acute stages of the disease, typical psoriatic lesions may develop in areas irritated by scratching or other nonspecific irritants (often in linear arrangement). This is called Koebner's phenomenon; it is not specific for psoriasis only. Special types of psoriasis are seen in certain skin regions.

Intertriginous psoriasis is found mostly in irritated areas of axillae and groins. *Hair growth* usually is not inhibited by the psoriatic process (Fig. 26). *Fingernails* (Fig. 27) and *toenails* may show characteristic changes, particularly stippling of the nail plate, brownish or whitish discoloration, accumulation of scale on the nail bed, and separation of the distal portion of the nail plate. Psoriasis of the *palms* and *soles* (Fig. 28) may present diagnostic difficulties if no other skin areas are involved. As in psoriatic changes of the nails, confusion with fungus infections must be avoided.

Pustular psoriasis is a rare clinical expression of the disease, characterized by the prevalence of microabscesses. Pustular psoriasis may be associated with chills, fever, arthritic pains, and a tendency to erythroderma (Zumbusch type) (Fig. 29). The Königsbeck-Barber-Ingram type, without systemic impairment, is usually limited to the distal extremities; it shows symmetrically arranged, grouped (but not confluent) pustules on red, scaly areas of the palms and soles, with psoriatic nail changes.

Occasionally, psoriasis may involve the small and large joints, particularly the distal phalanges of the fingers (Fig. 30). Recurrent attacks may produce deformity and ankylosis of the joints. *Arthropathic psoriasis* is often difficult to differentiate from other degenerative processes of the joints. Suggestive features are involvement of distal joints, typical X-ray findings and absence of rheumatoid factors in the serum.

The etiology and pathogenesis of psoriasis are not clear. A positive family history can be obtained in many patients.

Parapsoriasis

The parapsoriasis group has no direct relationship to psoriasis. It includes three rare varieties of widespread scaling eruptions on the trunk and extremities. Their etiology is unknown; they are notoriously resistant to treatment and follow a chronic course.

Lichenoid Parapsoriasis
(Pityriasis Lichenoides Chronica [Juliusberg])

New, small, red, round lichenoid lesions covered with fine scales develop next to older, paler, flat-topped lesions, each of which is covered with a grayish-white, thick scale (Fig. 31). Most lesions persist indefinitely. In some cases, a leukoderma remains after complete involution of the eruption.

Varioliform Parapsoriasis
(Pityriasis Lichenoides et Varioliformis Acuta [Mucha-Habermann])

In contrast to chronic forms of parapsoriasis, this disorder is probably due to primary vascular changes. It is now classified as an acute form of necrotizing vasculitis of unknown etiology. Following febrile infections, exanthematous eruptions appear with papulo-vesicular and hemorrhagic or necrotic lesions which often leave varioliform scars (Fig. 32).

Parapsoriasis en Plaques
(Erythrodermie pityriasique en plaques disseminées [Brocq])

This chronic disorder causes no discomfort. It is characterized by circumscribed yellowish to reddish-brown pseudoatrophic macular lesions with a very fine adherent scale. The plaques, which may reach the size of a hand, occur on trunk and extremities (Fig. 33). Differential diagnosis includes mycosis fungoides, which may have a similar onset. Increasing infiltration and pruritus are distinguishing features.

Retiform Parapsoriasis
(Parakeratosis Variegata [Unna])

Yellowish-red, flat-topped scaling papules become confluent in an annular or retiform pattern (Fig. 34). Late changes are atrophy, pigmentary disturbances, and teleangiectasias. Transition to mycosis fungoides has been observed.

Pityriasis Rosea (Gibert)

A relatively large, pink to fawn primary lesion ("herald patch"), usually located on the trunk, is followed by small, pityriasiform, faintly scaling, slightly erythematous, round to oval patches showing a typical crinkly scale ("collarette") at the border (Fig. 35). These secondary lesions are arranged in an exanthematous symmetrical pattern; their long axes run parallel to the lines of cleavage of the skin. They tend to heal spontaneously after several weeks, leaving immunity. The etiology of the disease is unknown, although many factors suggest an infectious origin.

Pityriasis Rubra Pilaris (Devergie)

This rare chronic dermatosis, which may occur in any age group, is characterized by disseminated erythematosquamous salmon-pink to reddish-brown plaques, with yellow to black, perifollicular, acuminate horny plugs (often pierced by a hairshaft), which produce a rough, grater-like surface (Figs. 36 and 37). The areas frequently involved are the extensor aspects of the extremities, dorsa of hands and fingers, flexor aspects of the joints, chest, face, neck, and abdomen. Generalized involvement, leaving characteristic irregular islands of skin intact, and transition to an exfoliative dermatitis are not uncommon. Palms and soles often are covered with fissured thick hyperkeratotic scaling masses (keratodermic sandal). The scalp may show severe pityriasiform scaling. Grayish-white patches of the oral mucosa, resembling the lesions of lichen planus, are rare. Instances suggesting a hereditary factor in the etiology of the disease have been reported.

Lichen Planus

Predilection sites of this disease are the flexor aspects of the upper extremities, the lateral aspects of the trunk, and the penis; the lips, the mucous membranes of the mouth (tongue), and (rarely) the face may be involved. The typical lesions, confined to the natural lines of the skin, are small, salmon-colored to bluish-lavender, polygonal, flat-topped papules with a smooth, shiny surface; they grow in number to form large patches and are usually associated with slight scaling and varying degrees of pruritus. In acute exanthematous exacerbations with more pronounced inflammation, the primary lesions have a more circular shape. Diascopy of the larger lesions with a glass slide reveals a lacy network of white streaks (Wickham's striae). New lesions often appear in linear fashion along scratch marks (Koebner's phenomenon) (Fig. 38). The following clinical variations of the disease are common.

Lichen planus annularis atrophicans is characterized by annular arrangement of lesions retaining the papular margin, while the center becomes atrophic.

Other variants show thick hyperkeratotic lesions (*lichen planus verrucosus*) on the anterior aspect of the lower legs (Fig. 39) and on the scrotum, or transformation of flat-topped nodules into pointed lesions (*lichen planus acuminatus*). *Bullous lichen planus* is usually surrounded by more typical lesions.

Involvement of mucous membranes, particularly of the buccal mucosa, may be seen in addition to or without skin changes. These lesions have a distinctive linear white lacy pattern (Fig. 40). On the tongue, they may simulate leukoplakia; on the lips, they have the appearance of a drop of paraffin.

A special follicular form of lichen planus is *lichen planopilaris* (Lassueur-Graham-Little syndrome) with cicatricial alopecia of the scalp (Figs. 41 and 42). Many cases of pseudopelade of Brocq are probably related to this type of lichen planus.

Acanthosis Nigricans

This dermatosis does not belong to the group of papulosquamous eruptions; it is not related to other skin diseases.

Symmetrically arranged, sharply defined, flesh-colored to brownish papules occur on the neck, corners of mouth, axillae, umbilical area, external genitals and chest. The skin markings become intensified; their surface later becomes deeply furrowed and verrucous (Fig. 43). Eventually, the lesions develop into irregular, hyperpigmented grayish to black patches of velvety papillary hypertrophy. The cause of this skin affection is unknown. Three forms may be distinguished.

The *malignant type* has about the same incidence in both sexes, and usually manifests itself in middle or late life.

It is rapidly progressive, often associated with pruritus, and has no typical sites of predilection. Endocrine disturbances are absent. The role of hereditary factors is not clear. Hyperpigmentation is pronounced. This type is associated with a high incidence of internal cancer, particularly abdominal adenocarcinomas. The skin lesions themselves never become malignant.

The *benign type* is a genodermatosis, probably related to endocrine changes during puberty. The disease predominantly affects the female sex, usually manifests itself in early childhood or at puberty, is rarely associated with pruritus, and has a high familial incidence. It may remain stationary or show spontaneous regression.

A third type, *pseudoacanthosis nigricans*, occurs in obese patients, usually before puberty, but may also start later. Endocrine disturbances associated with obesity, such as diabetes, thyroid dysfunction, or Cushing's syndrome, may be observed simultaneously. The skin changes show no progressive tendency, the lesions are less markedly pigmented. Predilection sites are axillae, neck and anogenital region.

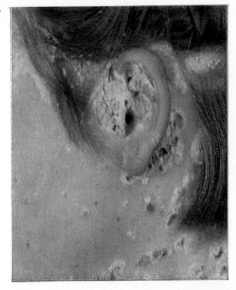

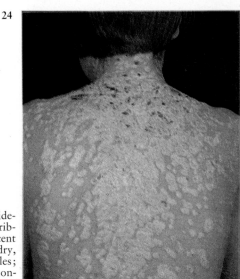

23 and 24 Psoriasis. Widespread, sharply circumscribed, discrete and coalescent patches with typical dry, silvery white thick scales; also early, small, salmon-red scaling papules.

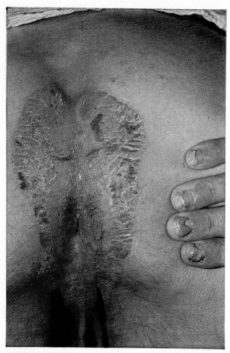

25 Psoriasis of the anal region and of the finger-nails. Sharply marginated lesions.

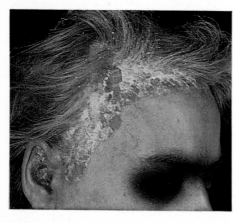

26 Psoriasis. Sharply marginated lesions of the scalp, forehead, and ears with thick white scales.

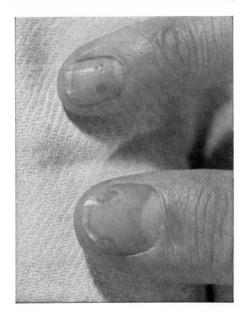

27 Psoriatic fingernails.
Brownish (oily) discoloration and punctate stippling of the nail plate.

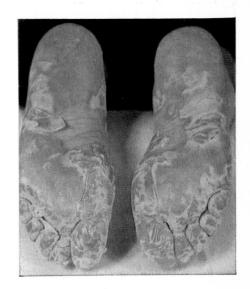

28 Psoriasis of soles.
Sharply marginated erythema with lamellar exfoliation.

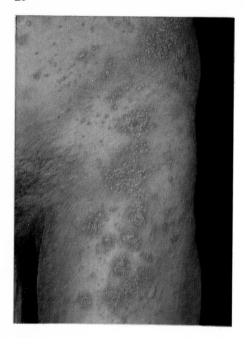

29 **Psoriasis; pustular type (von Zumbusch).** Erythematosquamous patches studded with small pustules. Severe constitutional symptoms.

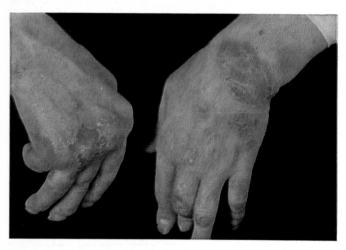

30 **Arthropathic psoriasis.** Deformity and ankylosis of the small joints, associated with typical skin lesions.

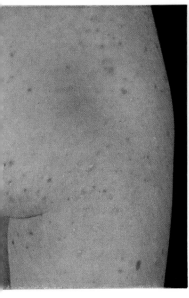

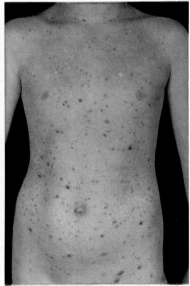

1   32

1 Lichenoid parapsoriasis (pity-riasis lichenoides chronica Julius-berg). Fresh, erythematous lichenoid lesions beside older flat-topped papules with grayish-white thick scales.

2 Acute varioliform parapsoriasis (pityriasis lichenoides et variolifor-mis acuta Mucha-Habermann). Papulovesicular hemorrhagic and necrotic lesions in exanthematous distribution.

3 Parapsoriasis en plaques (ery-throdermie pityriasique en plaques disseminées Brocq). Brownish-red plaques and irregularly outlined, pityriasiform, pseudoatrophic lesions. No infiltration, no pruritus.

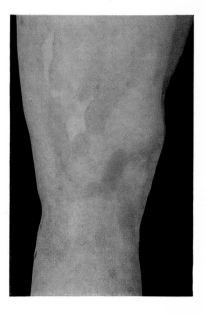

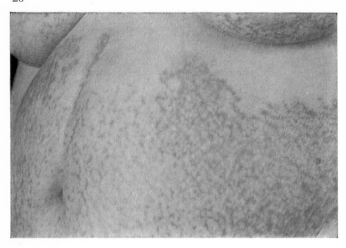

34 Retiform parapsoriasis (parakeratosis variegata Unna). Yellowish red, flat-topped scaling papules in annular and retiform arrangement with telangiectatic, atrophic, and pigmentary changes.

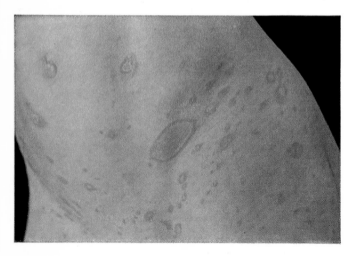

35 Pityriasis rosea. Primary plaque and secondary lesions. Typical marginal scaling (collarette).

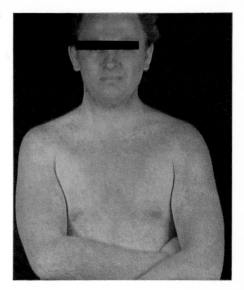

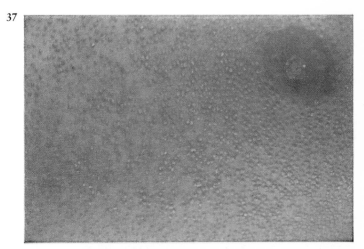

36 and 37   Pityriasis rubra pilaris (Devergie). Discrete pinhead-sized follicular papules with central horny plugs in symmetrical distribution, surrounded by islands of normal skin. Dorsa of fingers and hands are frequently involved; they show a typical "nutmeg grater" surface.

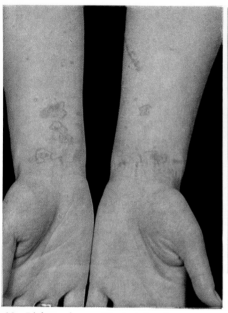

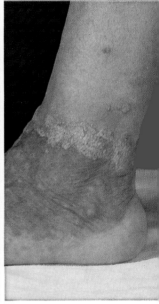

38 Lichen planus. Typical involvement of the wrists; salmon-colored to bluish-red, polygonal, flat-topped pruritic papules with a smooth shiny surface. Linear Koebner's phenomenon on the ulnar aspect of the left forearm.

39 Hypertrophic lichen planus. Elevated pruritic verrucous plaque on the lower leg.

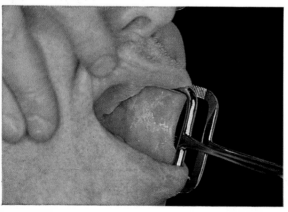

40 Lichen planus of oral mucosa. Distinctive linear and reticulate white lacy pattern.

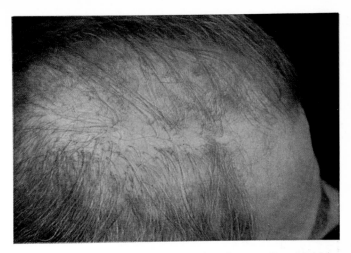

41 Lichen planopilaris (Graham-Little syndrome). Cicatricial alopecia of the scalp with follicular lesions of lichen planus.

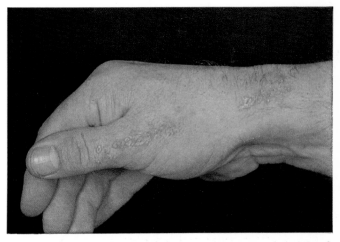

42 Lichen planopilaris (Graham-Little syndrome). Typical lichen planus lesions of the hand in same patient as in figure 41.

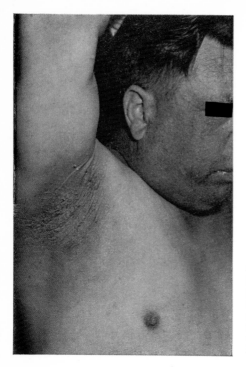

43 Acanthosis nigricans. Marked hyperpigmentation of axillae, face, and neck with hypertrophic axillary folds, characteristic of malignant type. No tumor has been found yet in this patient.

Dermatitis-Eczema Group

Dermatitis-Eczema

The terms dermatitis and eczema are used for a characteristic sequence of inflammatory changes of the epidermis and upper dermis which can be induced by a variety of irritants, allergens and other factors. In the past, the term eczema was used for different chronic forms of dermatitis. In modern usage, it is meaningless without qualifying adjectives and should best be avoided.

The characteristic sequence of dermatitic skin changes consists mainly of erythematous and edematous patches, followed by papules, vesicles, and oozing. Mild to severe pruritus is usually present. Scaling, erosions, crusts, and circumscribed lichenification are seen in later stages of the disease.

Contact Dermatitis

Skin changes in contact dermatitis start in areas of contact with the irritating or allergenic agent. The reaction is usually localized and limited to the area of exposure. Two main types of contact dermatitis can be differentiated. *Primary irritant (toxic) contact dermatitis* may occur in any individual, without prior exposure, shortly after contact with an offending substance of sufficient strength. *Allergic contact dermatitis* occurs only in sensitized individuals. Repeated exposure to the same agent is necessary to induce dermatitic changes which appear after an incubation period of varying length. Once the patient is sensitized, even minimal contact may cause exacerbation. *Id reactions*, possibly due to autosensitization, can be seen in severe cases of contact dermatitis in regions distant from the original contact area, often in widespread distribution.

Common contact allergens and diagnostic methods are described in the discussion of cutaneous allergy.

Nummular Dermatitis

This common clinical variety of the dermatitis-eczema group is characterized by pruritic, coin-like (nummular), oozing patches, frequently located on the extensor surfaces of arms, hands, and legs. Sometimes it is related to an exacerbation of other chronic eczematous processes, particularly of the lower legs. In patients with an atopic history, it is considered an exudative form of neurodermatitis (in contrast to the dry form, lichen simplex chronicus); in other patients it represents a clinically distinct form of contact dermatitis.

Seborrheic Dermatitis (Unna)

Perifollicular, pinhead-sized, erythematous pink or yellowish lesions which grow into macular patches appear on the scalp and face, in the retroauricular, presternal and interscapular areas, in the umbilical region, in the gluteal crease, axillae and genital area (Fig. 44). The dermatitis is usually confined to areas richly supplied with sebaceous glands. Round or oval, polycyclic, and punctate perifollicular lesions may arise simultaneously or in succession. As the originally pinkish macules increase in size, they assume a yellowish coloring, and are covered with greasy scales and dirty yellow crusts. Typical eczematous changes (papulovesicles, exudative lesions) are seen only occasionally, and then only in the marginal areas of the lesions. Increased sebum production and hyperhidrosis provide the basis for microbial action and inflammatory changes, which lead to sensitization and thus help maintain the dermatitis. A lowered resistance to superficial bacterial infection favors the formation and persistence of seborrheic dermatitis.

Atopic Dermatitis (Coca-Sulzberger)

(Disseminated Neurodermatitis Brocq)
(Prurigo diathésique Besnier)

Atopic dermatitis often starts in infancy, affecting the lateral aspects of the face; two-thirds of the cases of so-called "infantile eczema" are early manifestations of atopic dermatitis. There is usually a family or personal history of atopy, e.g., atopic dermatitis, urticaria, asthma, or hay fever.

The typical facial lesions are followed in childhood by eczematous eruptions involving the flexor surfaces of the arms and legs, the dorsa of the hands, and the wrists (Fig. 45). Lichenification, the principal criterion of atopic dermatitis, is predominant. The disease reaches its maximum in extent and severity during the second and third decades, then gradually subsides. Each episode starts with violent attacks of pruritus, probably related to excessive dryness of the skin. These attacks, which particularly occur at nighttime, provoke furious scratching which promotes lichenification and secondary infection of the skin. The lichenified skin of the forehead, antecubital and popliteal fossae, the characteristic frustrated facial expression, the broken-off lateral portions of the eyebrows (Herthoge's sign), and the atopic pleats of the eyelids are typical diagnostic features (Fig. 46).

Not infrequently, ophthalmologic examination with a slit lamp reveals a cataract. The most serious, potentially fatal complication of atopic dermatitis is superinfection with herpes simplex or vaccinia virus, which has a tendency to become generalized. Both complications, *eczema herpeticum* and *eczema vaccinatum*, will be discussed in the chapter on virus infections of the skin.

Lichen Simplex Chronicus (Vidal)
(Circumscribed Neurodermatitis Brocq)

This severely pruritic disorder is a separate form of neurodermatitis, easily distinguishable from the generalized (disseminated, diffuse) type. The striate lesions or solitary circumscribed round to ovoid lichenified patches are usually seen in middle-aged patients, primarily on the inner aspects of the thighs, the extensor aspects of the lower legs, and in the occipital-nuchal region. The lichenified areas are the result of constant scratching and rubbing.

Prurigo Nodularis (Hyde)

This rare disease is closely related to circumscribed neurodermatitis. Isolated dome-shaped, dark, itching nodules which may reach a diameter of 1 to 2 cm. occur on extremities (Fig. 47), in the face, and occasionally on the trunk. The surrounding skin may be normal or lichenified. The nodules usually show an excoriated and verrucous surface.

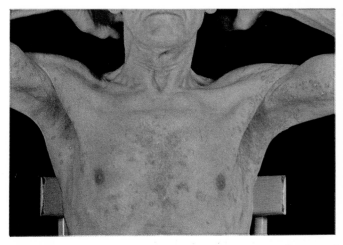

44 Seborrheic dermatitis. Typical involvement of sternal area and axillae.

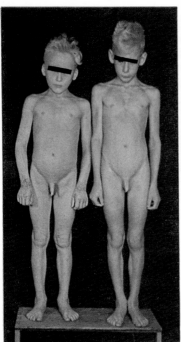

45 Atopic dermatitis in brothers. Dry lichenified eczematous eruption of the face and extremities.

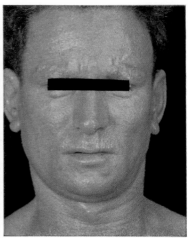

46 Atopic dermatitis. Erythema, scaling, lichenification, and loss of lateral portion of eyebrows due to rubbing and scratching.

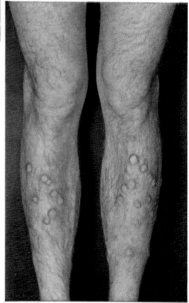

47 Prurigo nodularis (Hyde). Dome-shaped pruritic nodules with verrucous surface.

Cutaneous Allergy

Allergy is an acquired specific alteration in the capacity to react, brought about by interaction of an antigen with its specific antibody. Anaphylaxis, idiosyncrasy, hypersensitivity reaction are medical terms of historical importance; these responses are now classified as different types of allergic reaction. The concept of immunity has become somewhat separated from the more comprehensive concept of allergy; both are antigen-antibody mechanisms, respectively leading to pathogenic (allergy) and nonpathogenic (immunity) responses of the organism. *Antigens* (allergens) are substances which induce the formation of specific proteins (antibodies). The ability of antigens to combine with their antibodies produces complex antigen-antibody reactions, which are the fundamental mechanism of *allergy*.

Two types of allergic reactions are recognized.

1. *Immediate reaction:* In the presence of serum antibodies, clinical symptoms appear within minutes after introduction of the specific antigen (e.g., serum sickness, bronchial asthma, urticaria, reactions to parasites, and some drug allergies). Circulating antibodies may be demonstrated with the Prausnitz-Küstner reaction.

2. *Delayed reaction:* Clinical symptoms manifest themselves after 12 to 48 hours (e.g., allergy of infection and allergic contact dermatitis). A number of substances may elicit *allergic skin reactions* (Figs 48—62), such as morbilliform, scarlatiniform, urticarial, hemorrhagic, erythema multiforme-like, and fixed drug eruptions (which consistently occur at the same site following oral or parenteral administration of the antigen).

Drug Allergy

Virtually any drug can be allergenic. The most common agents are: antibiotics, sulfonamides, p-aminosalicylic acid, oral antidiabetic agents (carbutamide, tolbutamide), local anesthetics (p-aminobenzoic acid ethyl ester, procaine), phenothiazines, barbiturates, hydantoin derivates, carbamide, radiological contrast media containing iodine, aminophenazone, aniline derivates (phenacetin), salicylic acid derivatives, quinine, quinidine, phenolphthalein, mercury compounds, antithyroid agents (thio-, methylthio-, propylthiouracil), arsenobenzene derivatives, and antihistaminics.

Food Allergy

The most important *food allergens* are fish, crustaceans, pork, cow's milk, cheese, eggs, chocolate, honey, strawberries, nuts, corn, tomatoes and citrus fruits. Acute urticaria is often caused by these foods. Erythema multiforme, atopic dermatitis and acne vulgaris are occasionally related to food factors.

Contact Allergy

Common *contact allergens* are chromates, nickel compounds, mercurial salts, arsenicals, aromatic amines (p-phenylene diamine, aniline), azo dyes, halogenated aromatic nitro- and amino-compounds, turpentine, divalent phenols bearing aliphatic substitutes, *tetramethylthiuram disulfide*, *mercaptobenzothiazol*, phenol, formaldehyde, resins, epoxy resins, *methacrylates*, thioglycolates, various cosmetics, penta*decylcatechol* (poison ivy, poison oak, poison sumac) and exotic hardwoods.

Skin Tests

Diagnosis of allergy is facilitated by a number of easily performed cutaneous tests. *Patch tests* are eminently useful in delayed reactions (contact dermatitis); they carry the slight risk of other local reactions and exacerbation of the existing contact dermatitis. The suspected allergen is applied in proper dilution to the back or upper arm for one to two days. A typical dermatitic reaction after 24 to 48 hours indicates a positive test. Patch tests should not be applied in acute stages of dermatitis. *Intradermal skin tests* for immediate reactions are difficult to interpret; systemic allergic reactions of other shock organs (e.g., bronchial asthma) cannot be avoided and may be fatal. Other methods, such as passive transfer of antibodies by the Prausnitz-Küstner technique, and the exposition test, should be performed only under the supervision of experienced physicians.

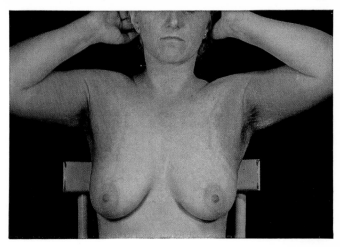

48 Allergic contact dermatitis. Induced by formalin impregnated garments.

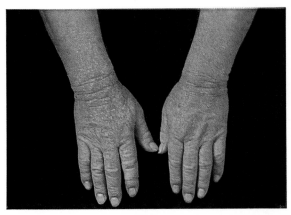

49 Allergic contact dermatitis. Occupational dermatitis due to cement (chromates) in a bricklayer. Chronic dry eczematous eruption of the hands.

40

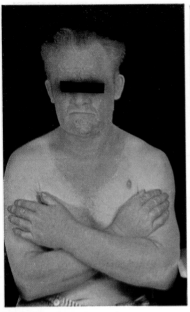

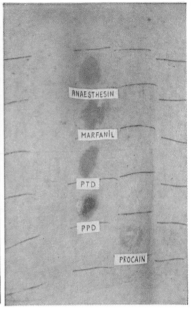

50 Allergic contact dermatitis. Due to treatment with a topical anesthetic cream. (Anaesthesin).

51 Positive patch test. To Anaesthesin and other substances with aromatic amino groups in para-position (group allergy).

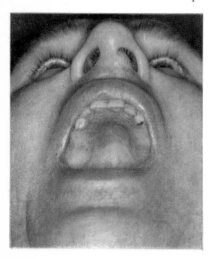

52 Allergic reaction of oral mucosa. Induced by monomeric methacrylates (dentures).

41

53 Positive patch test. Erythematous reaction due to plastic component of dentures (cf. Fig. 52).

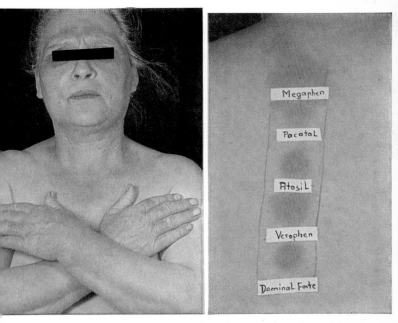

and 55 **Contact dermatitis due to phenothiazine derivative.** Positive h test. Typical group allergy.

42

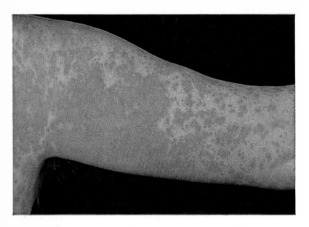

56 Confluent macular drug eruption. Due to a hydantoin derivative.

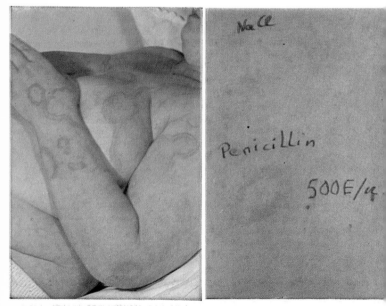

57 Urticaria. Due to parenteral administration of penicillin.

58 Positive intracutaneous test. Wheal with peripheral erythematou flare and pseudopods following injec tion of diluted penicillin.

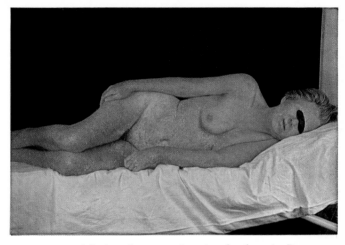

59 Severe exfoliative drug eruption (erythroderma). Due to a pyrazolone derivative.

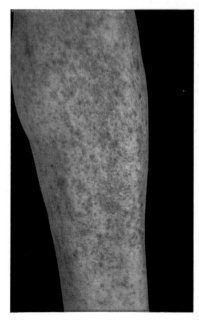

60 Purpuric drug eruption. Following ingestion of a quinine-containing cold remedy.

44

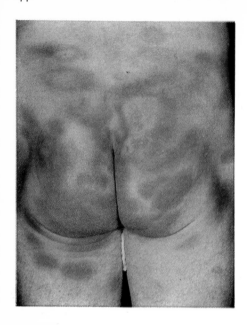

61 Fixed drug eruption.
Due to barbiturates.

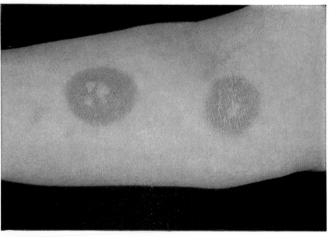

62 Fixed drug eruption. Due to analgesic containing pyrazolone. Round, erythematous, and hyperpigmented patches, recurrent in identical location.

Infectious Diseases

Micrococcal Infections

Most purulent skin diseases are due to infections by streptococci or staphylococci. Principal portals of entry are the hair follicles in adults and the sweat ducts in infants and children. Lack of hygiene and increased perspiration due to high humidity produce epidermal changes which facilitate invasion by the micrococci. Lymphogenous and hematogenous infections are rare. Important factors determining the course and development of micrococcal infections of the skin are pathogenicity, virulence and contagiosity of the microorganisms, and the predisposition or resistance of the host.

Pathogenic organisms can be identified by means of specific culture media, and their sensitivity to antibiotics can be determined by special techniques.

Classification of micrococcal skin diseases is a controversial problem. The most widely recognized systems are those of Darier, who attempts to classify pyodermas according to the depth of the lesions, and of Jadassohn, who takes into consideration etiology, relationship of the skin changes to the skin appendages, site of the lesions (epidermal, dermal, or hypodermal), and extent of the infection.

Follicular Impetigo (Bockhart)

This superficial micrococcal infection (usually due to coagulase-positive staphylococci, Micrococcus pyogenes variatio aureus) is limited to the follicular ostia; it may be idiopathic, but more frequently it occurs as a complication of existing dermatoses or after application of tar products, oils, and moist occlusive dressings.

The primary lesion is a pinhead-sized or larger, thin-walled, dome-shaped pustule filled with yellowish-green pus, often pierced by a hair and surrounded by a narrow, slightly infiltrated red halo (Fig. 63); not infrequently, this primary lesion later develops into a furuncle. The disease can be differentiated from a deep folliculitis by the absence of edema, infiltration, and pain. Vacciniform pustulosis, a typical ostiofolliculitis, also belongs to this category.

Furuncle

A furuncle is a deep folliculitis and perifolliculitis of bacterial origin, with infiltration extending into the cutis and subcutis; this, in association with the concomitant edema, produces severe pain and tenderness. The furuncle may develop on the basis of a follicular impetigo, but more frequently it originates from a firm, painful infiltrate in the depth of the follicle. Systemic symptoms are rare. After perforation and discharge of the pus and central core (follicular and perifollicular necrosis), the furuncle eventually heals, leaving a scar.

Carbuncle

A carbuncle is formed by coalescing follicular and perifollicular necroses of several adjacent furuncles. The lesion is seen more frequently in older patients, predominantly in males. The local process is of considerable depth, the general health is sometimes impaired.
The appearance of furuncles or carbuncles immediately calls for measures to rule out diabetes mellitus.

Sycosis Barbae
(Folliculitis Barbae)

This rare disorder is more common in bearded men. It presents an extremely polymorphous clinical picture (Fig. 64). On a background of reddened, edematous skin, discrete papules or pustules, each pierced by a hair shaft and surrounded by an inflammatory halo, are seen next to erosions, perforated pustules discharging pus, and larger inflamed nodules from which hairs imbedded in a gelatinous mass may be plucked without pain.
The preferred area is the beard (barber's itch), but eyelashes, eyebrows, scalp, as well as axillary, pubic and body hair may also be involved. The causative organisms are usually staphylococci, sometimes streptococci. The disease does not tend to heal spontaneously; its therapy is time-consuming and taxes the patience of both physician and patient.

Acne Necrotica (Hebra)
(Acne Varioliformis)

In contrast to acne vulgaris, this rare chronic, recurrent condition occurs in middle age; also in contrast, comedones or cysts are absent. On the forehead, the hairline, the temporal area, the scalp (rarely on the face, chest, and back), discrete bright red papules and pustules appear, with a small disk-shaped necrotic area developing in the center (Fig. 65). A round, depressed, superficial scar remains after the crust has fallen off. The lesions are not limited to the hair follicles. Bacteriologic examination regularly reveals staphylococci and streptococci.

Hidradenitis Suppurativa
(Apocrine Sweat Gland Abscesses)

Painful confluent abscesses of apocrine sweat glands of the axillary or anogenital region usually develop from small red nodular subcutaneous infiltrations or from a folliculitis. Coalescing nodules often form elongated masses parallel to the body folds, with purulent draining sinus tracts.

Pemphigus Neonatorum
(Impetigo Neonatorum)

This rare, acute, often fatal bullous variety of impetigo occurs in infants in poor health in the postnatal period (Fig. 66). In many cases, it can be traced to impetigo contagiosa of older siblings, or to paronychia of the person attending the infant.
Another rare variety of severe infantile pyoderma is *dermatitis exfoliativa neonatorum* (Ritter von Rittershain), which shows coalescent flaccid bullae, widespread exfoliation, and severe systemic symptoms.

Impetigo Contagiosa

This common type of pyoderma is caused by various organisms. It is highly contagious only to infants and does not leave scars. Small yellow pustules with an intense erythematous base which dry up rapidly, leaving heavy, stuck-on, honey-colored crusts, are often caused by streptococci (Fig. 67), whereas shallow, rapidly spreading bullae coalescing into circinate, fast-drying and scaling lesions with flat brownish crusts sometimes are due to staphylococci. However, mixed infections are more common.

Ecthyma

Ecthyma is a deep variety of impetigo. It is charcterized by large erosive or ulcerative lesions covered with thick purulent crusts. These lesions are more common in areas with diminished blood supply or in debilitated patients.

Erysipelas

This superficial streptococcal cellulitis starts with high temperatures and chills, and is characterized by tender, sharply circumscribed, shiny, hot, red, edematous plaques (Fig. 68). The lesions spread with raised advancing borders and red lymphangitic streaks. Fever, malaise, and systemic symptoms are common, but may be absent in older patients.

Vesicular, bullous, gangrenous, and phlegmonous variants of erysipelas also occur.

Chronic recurrent erysipelas (as well as recurrent thrombophlebitis) gradually leads to *elephantiasis nostras* which is characterized by a chronic lymphedema and pachyderma.

Bacterial Paronychia

Purulent, recurrent, often chronic inflammation of the tissues around the nail frequently is due to prolonged maceration, or follows hangnails or vigorous manicuring of the nail folds. The disorder is more common in women. The nail folds are red, swollen, tense, and painful. In acute cases, a small amount of pus often can be expressed from the tender areas.

Noncoccal Infections

Anthrax

Bacillus anthracis infections usually occur in cattle and sheep, but also in hogs, fowl, horses, and deer. Man is infected either by direct contact with these animals, or by handling their hides or contaminated soil. Occupations especially exposed to this infection are farmers, veterinarians, butchers, longshoremen, leather and wool handlers, laboratory personnel, and physicians.

After an incubation period of 2 to 8 days, a red maculopapular lesion appears at the portal of entry of the pathogenic organism (usually hands or fingers). Two days later, a flaccid, serous, later hemorrhagic bulla (*pustula maligna*) develops in the center of the lesion (Fig. 69). The surrounding area becomes intensely infiltrated and shows a reddish-brown to livid coloring; the regional lymph nodes are enlarged. The center of the hemorrhagic bulla dries up to form a painless ulcer covered with a characteristic black adherent *eschar*. Occasionally, progressive edematous infiltrations lead to invasion of the blood stream by the organism. The resulting *septicemia* is associated with severe systemic manifestations, and has a grave prognosis. Patients afflicted with anthrax should be kept isolated.

Erysipeloid (Rosenbach)

After an incubation period of 1 to 2 days, a typical violaceous to red, well defined, inflammatory edematous lesion appears at the site of inoculation with swine erysipelas (Erysipelothrix rhusiopathiae) following minor trauma to the hands or fingers (Fig. 70). The lesions progress rapidly in arciform or gyrate configurations with a tendency to central clearing. The manifestations are considerably less acute than those of erysipelas. Systemic symptoms are usually absent; a generalized infection with endocarditis and joint pains is very rare. The disease is contracted through the handling of meat from infected animals, particularly fish, shellfish, venison or poultry, or through contact with decaying wood or contaminated soil.

Cutaneous Leishmaniasis
(Oriental Sore, Aleppo Boil)

After an incubation period of a few days to several months, the protozoal parasite (Leishmania tropica), usually transmitted by mosquito bites (Phlebotomus sandflies), produces small, itching, purple papules which gradually develop into nodules or indurated disk-like lesions with brownish marginal zones (Fig. 71). Sharply circumscribed, round punched-out ulcers with indurated borders are frequently seen. Infiltrated lesions may simulate a syphilitic chancre; crusted ulcers are suggestive of pyodermas. The disease is common in the Middle East and in tropical areas of Asia, Africa, and America. It is limited to the skin, and occurs principally on exposed areas of children and young adults. Spontaneous remission often occurs after several months, leaving immunity. Diagnostic tests include demonstration of the parasite in smears obtained by curetting, and a delayed response to the leishmanin test.

Mucocutaneous Leishmaniasis
(South American Leishmaniasis)

This tropical disease caused by Leishmania braziliensis is predominant in South America, particularly in wooded regions. The skin lesions resemble those of cutaneous leishmaniasis; in addition, there is a moderate tendency to involve the mucous membranes of nose, mouth and pharynx. The diagnosis is established by skin scrapings and a delayed reaction to the Montenegro test.

Tuberculosis

Cutaneous tuberculosis rarely is seen in the United States of America. All skin changes produced by Mycobacterium tuberculosis (Koch) are referred to as tuberculosis of the skin. Bacteriologic examination of the lesions usually reveals the human, less frequently the bovine type of the mycobacterium. Despite their common etiology, the clinical manifestations of cutaneous tuberculosis vary widely due to different allergic responses.

The course of the disease depends largely on the patient's biologic reactions. This specific allergy is easily determined by percutaneous and intracutaneous tests (von Pirquet, Moro, Mendel-Mantoux). The following responses are possible:

Anergic response: The organism fails to form antibodies either because it has not yet had contact with mycobacteria, or because it has exhausted its resources (cachexia). Invasion and propagation of the bacteria are not checked by the patient's defense mechanisms. Tuberculin reaction is negative.

Normergic response: Antibody formation of intermediate intensity signifies an equilibrium of host and pathogenic organism. Tuberculin reaction is positive ($1:10^4$).

Hyperergic response: The pathogen produces violent acute inflammatory reactions to the point of ulceration and necrosis. Tuberculin reaction is strongly positive (up to $1:10^7$).
Other factors determining the clinical course of skin tuberculosis are the pathways used by the mycobacterium (disseminated through blood or lymph channels, by contiguity or exogenous infection) and the zone of the skin where the microorganism eventually settles.

Primary Inoculation Tuberculosis

The tuberculous primary complex (tuberculous chancre) of the skin, consisting of a nodule slowly evolving into an indurated ulcer, occurs almost exclusively in infants and young children. Areas of predilection are the face and extremities. Prominent regional lymphadenopathy is a characteristic finding (Fig. 72). The incubation period is 2 to 4 weeks. BCG vaccination also may produce the picture of a cutaneous tuberculous primary complex.

Tuberculosis Cutis Orificialis

(Tuberculosis Ulcerosa Cutis et Mucosae)

In a completely anergic state (negative tuberculin test), highly contagious, rapidly ulcerating, indolent skin lesions may occur in the preterminal stage of visceral tuberculosis, involving areas contiguous to mucocutaneous junctions (Fig. 73). These lesions are produced by massive auto-inoculation of mycobacteria excreted with body fluids.

Lupus Vulgaris
(Tuberculosis Cutis Luposa)

This is the most common form of cutaneous tuberculosis, manifesting a normergic state of allergy (Figs. 74—80). It can be produced only by superinfection, usually endogenously, i.e., by hematogenous dissemination. In the course of months or years, an isolated, soft, red or yellowish-brown nodule slowly develops into the characteristic chronic annular scaling plaque. The diagnostically significant nodule, occurring primarily on the face, is comprised histologically of a collection of typical tubercles. On diascopic examination, the area is blanched, revealing pinhead-sized round nodules of apple jelly color (Fig. 75). With a fine probe, the necrotic infiltrate is easily penetrated; the resulting bleeding ceases readily.
Different clinical types of lupus vulgaris are described in the legends to the illustrations.

Scrofuloderma
(Tuberculosis Cutis Colliquativa)

A form of cutaneous tuberculosis based on a normergic response in children, scrofuloderma usually derives from a tuberculous infection of the lymph nodes or bones underlying the affected skin area. Less frequently, primary subcutaneous lesions are produced by hematogenous dissemination. Characteristic clinical features are slowly enlarging lymph nodes (usually of the neck) which gradually become adherent to the skin, necrotize, and discharge thin yellowish-green pus through fistulous openings, leaving bizarre corded hypertrophic scars (Fig. 81).

Tuberculosis Verrucosa Cutis

This condition, which is also called „prosector's wart," usually occurs in the hands, and has its highest incidence in persons handling tuberculous material (pathologists, veterinarians, butchers, etc.). The lesions are produced by exogenous infection in a normergic state of allergy. They start as red papules which become crusted and may develop into large vegetative, verrucous plaques with slight purulent discharge (Fig. 82).

Tuberculids

In a markedly hyperergic state of allergy, hematogenous dissemination may procedure symmetrically arranged lesions referred to as tuberculids (Darier). Demonstration of mycobacteria in the skin has been reported. Local circulatory deficiencies may play a significant pathogenetic rôle in *erythema induratum Bazin* and *papulonecrotic tuberculids.* Other tuberculids are *lichen scrofulosorum (tuberculosis cutis lichenoides)* and *tuberculosis miliaris disseminata faciei.* In rare cases, tuberculids may simulate granuloma annulare, erythema nodosum, or lichen nitidus.

Lichen Scrofulosorum (Hebra)
(Tuberculosis Cutis Lichenoides)

Small, skin-colored or pink to reddish-brown, flat-topped, firm follicular papules appear at first in scattered isolated lesions, later as patches or lichenoid papules, on the trunk of children with systemic tuberculosis. The lichenoid lesions often bear fine scales or horny plugs (Fig. 83). Spontaneous remissions and recurrences have been reported.

Papulonecrotic Tuberculid
(Tuberculosis Papulonecrotica)

Indolent purplish papules, pustules, necroses, and varioloform scars on the extensor aspects of the distal extremities (Fig. 84) or the face are typical of this disorder, which often takes a chronic, recurrent course. The disease occurs in adults with an active form of tuberculosis elsewhere, indicating a hyperergic response.

Erythema Induratum (Bazin)
(Tuberculosis Indurativa Cutanea et Subcutanea)

This type of hyperergic tuberculosis of the skin occurs most commonly in younger women with peripheral circulatory disorders. Solitary or grouped indolent nodular infiltrates are localized on the borderline between cutis and subcutis, especially of the calves of the legs. The overlying skin turns bluish-red, the lesions ulcerate and eventually heal with scar formation. Usually, all stages of the chronic recurrent disease are seen simultaneously in one patient (Fig. 85).

Lupus Miliaris Disseminatus Faciei (Tilbury-Fox)
(Tuberculosis Miliaris Disseminata Faciei)

Small, soft, noncoalescing dome-shaped papules of pale red to yellowish-brown or brownish-red coloring occur bilaterally, mainly in the face of adult patients (Fig. 86). Diascopy shows "apple jelly" infiltrates. The papular lesions may heal with scar formation. Clinically, this rare disorder is more closely related to papulonecrotic tuberculid than to lupus vulgaris, and may therefore be classified as a tuberculid. The immunobiological state associated with this disease also suggests its relationship to the tuberculid group.

Leprosy (Hansen)

This mildly contagious, chronic infectious disease, which has been known for several millenia, is caused by Mycobacterium leprae (Hansen). Millions are still suffering from this disease, though it is rare in the United States. Two clinical types are known. The more malignant, contagious *lepromatous leprosy* (nodular leprosy), is characterized by nodular infiltrates (lepromas), which often start as erythematous macules with diffuse borders. These macules are localized mostly on the ear lobes (Fig. 87), nose, supraorbital region (leonine facies) (Fig. 88), elbows, and buttocks. Scrapings of these lesions show mycobacteria in great numbers. The nasal mucous membranes become involved at an early stage of the disease; the lepromas ulcerate, causing epistaxis, perforation of the septum, and further dissemination of the organisms with the nasal secretions. Internal organs, lymph nodes, eyes, and bones also may become involved. Necrotic sequestration and mutilitation may occur, especially on the hands and feet. The lepromin (Mitsuda) reaction is negative (anergic response). Erythema nodosum-like reactions are common.

The second, more frequent, and relatively benign type, *tuberculoid leprosy* (maculo-anesthetic leprosy), is noninfectious and may heal spontaneously if living conditions are adequate. Large erythemato-squamous, slightly raised, often circinate anhidrotic plaques are arranged in an asymmetrical pattern (Fig. 89) on the face, extremities, and buttocks. The sharply outlined anesthetic macular lesions are often hypopigmented and show central clearing. Involvement of the mucous membranes is rare. Progressive neurological involvement with neuritis and fusiform thickening of ulnar and peroneal nerves is typical. The disease does not spread to internal organs. The lepromin test is positive; bacilli cannot always be demonstrated.

Atypical forms of an intermediate nature are referred to as *indeterminate types of leprosy*. The Mitsuda reaction may be negative or positive. Mycobacteria are sparse or absent. The *borderline* or *dimorphic type* is not stable and may change into other types.

Fungus Diseases

(Dermatomycoses)

Infectious diseases of the skin, hair, and nails, when produced essentially by ringworm fungi and yeasts, are referred to as dermatomycoses. The causative organisms are easily demonstrable microscopically. Examination of scrapings treated with 10 per cent potassium hydroxide yields positive results in a high percentage of cases. Hyphae and spores can be visualized; however, identification of the type of fungus, or even differentiation between dermatophytes and yeasts, is not possible by this method. This must be done with the aid of special culture media.

Tineas
(Dermatophytoses)

Fungi penetrating into the upper epidermal layers produce a small, red, itching and scaling spot which grows centrifugally. The marginal zone of the lesion is occupied by numerous small vesicles which soon become pustular (Fig. 90—101). While the central portion of the eruption tends to heal spontaneously, the raised marginal zone spreads in a ring-like pattern (Fig. 90). An obsolete term for superficial tineas is trichophytia superficialis, which was used to differentiate it from deeper dermatophytic infections (tinea profunda, trichophytia profunda).

Tineas involving deeper layers of the skin usually develop from long-standing superficial tineas. Ostiofollicular pustules, folliculitis, perifolliculitis, and necrotic degeneration may occur. The lesions coalesce into verruciform or dome-shaped, soft succulent tumors. Upon application of pressure, pus drains from numerous openings as from a sponge. In the past, this type was often seen in the beard area (sycosis barbae) (Fig. 92).

Deep follicular fungus infections of the lower legs are often seen in women after they have shaved their legs. They are characterized by livid, itching, nodular granulomas which may extend into the subcutaneous tissue (Fig. 93). Hyphae and spores are usually demonstrable when affected hairs are treated with potassium hydroxide.

Some special clinical types of tineas, which are due to regional differences, will be discussed in greater detail.

Tinea Unguium
(Onychomycosis)

This infection usually involves isolated nails, rarely all of the fingernails or toenails. The dermatophytes grow in the nail plate, which becomes opaque, brittle, cracked, and partially separated from the nail bed, and shows a dirty yellowish-gray discoloration (Fig. 94). The nail infection is usually associated with a fungus infection of the surrounding skin (frequently caused by Trichophyton rubrum).

Tinea Cruris
(Tinea Marginatum Hebra)

This chronic pruritic fungus infection, which spreads peripherally in polycyclic configurations with a slightly elevated border and scaling center (Fig. 95) occurs predominantly in the genitocrural area. The fungi most frequently isolated from these lesions are Trichophyton rubrum, Trichophyton mentagrophytes, and Epidermophyton floccosum.

Tinea Pedis et Manus

This infection of the hands and feet is often caused by trichophyton species. Clinically, a dyshidrotic (Fig. 96), a squamous-hyperkeratotic (Fig. 97) and an intertriginous (Fig. 98) type can be distinguished.

Dermatophytids

Sudden macular, lichenoid, or vesicular eruptions may be associated with systemic symptoms (fever, chills, headaches) as the result of a hyperergic state of allergy. The trichophytin test is strongly positive in dilutions up to 1:300 (Fig. 99). Another important criterion for the diagnosis of a dermatophytid is the presence of an acute inflammatory ringworm infection elsewhere.

Tinea Capitis

Tinea capitis used to occur epidemically in children. The scalp shows round or oval, sharply defined lesions covered with pityriasiform scales. In the affected area, the hairs are broken off at a length of about 1 mm (Fig. 100).
In rare cases, the skin is reddened or moderately infiltrated. In addition to the scalp, skin areas covered with vellus hair and nails may be affected. Under Wood's light, the tinea lesions or epilated hairs infested with the fungus show a typical bright yellowish-green fluorescence. The infection may be caused by Microsporum audouini, M. canis (often contracted from animals), or M. gypseum. *Kerion celsi* occurs as an allergic reaction in severe cases of tinea capitis in form of sharply defined partially alopecic soft succulent granulomatous areas with numerous purulent draining openings (Fig. 91).

Tinea Versicolor
(Pityriasis Versicolor)

This frequently ecountered superficial fungus infection caused by Malassezia furfur is even more common in hot, humid climates. Sharply defined confluent, round or irregular, yellowish to brownish or depigmented, slightly scaling patches usually involve the upper trunk, neck, and upper arms (Fig. 101). The scaling becomes more evident after gentle scraping.

Erythrasma

Small, red, sharply defined lesions, coalescing into brownish or reddish-brown patches with very faint scaling (Figs. 102 and 103), are seen on the inner aspect of the thighs adjacent to the scrotum or labia, in the axillary and submammary areas and between the fourth and fifth toes. The involved areas show coral red fluorescence under Wood's light. The causative organism was originally named Nocardia minutissima; it can be visualized under oil immersion. Recent investigations indicate that it is a bacterium and not a fungus.

Candidiasis
(Moniliasis)

Yeast infections have gained increasing clinical importance in recent years. Diseases caused by yeasts and yeast-like fungi are common in intertriginous areas; they also can involve mucous membranes and internal organs. Interdigital monilial infections of the toes and onychomycosis of the toes and fingers cannot be distinguished clinically from similar dermatoses caused by dermatophytes. Differentiation of the microorganisms is possible only by the use of culture media.

Typical yeast infections of the skin are *interdigital moniliasis* (erosio interdigitalis blastomycetica), *monilial intertrigo, monilial paronychia, thrush* (moniliasis of the mouth) (Fig. 104) and *monilial vaginitis. Monilial granulomas* rarely occur on skin and mucous membranes. Id reactions (candidids) are not uncommon.

Chromoblastomycosis

This disease is seen mainly in tropical and subtropical climates. Ulcerated, verrucous or papillomatous growths form on a papular base (Fig. 105), especially on the lower extremities. The causative organisms (Phialophora verrucosa, Hormodendrum pedrosoi, Hormodendrum compactum, and other fungi) invade the tissue through small abrasions. They are easily demonstrable in smears and histologic preparations.

Actinomycosis

Actinomyces israeli, the microorganism causing actinomycosis, is a bacterial organism rather than a fungus. The chronic infiltrating inflammatory process is most common in the cervicofacial area, starting on the oral mucosa or the tonsils. Other forms involve the thoracic or abdominal area. Characteristic clinical features are mildly tender woody induration, abscess formation, ulceration, sinus tracts, and purulent discharge (Fig. 106). The diagnosis is confirmed by the presence of tiny whitish or yellowish "sulfur granules" (masses of fungi) which often can be visualized macroscopically.

Viral Diseases

Viruses cannot be cultured in synthetic media; they multiply only in living cells. Dermatologic research has yielded considerable insight into the various types of viruses and their relationship to the host cells. Virus diseases occur in men, in animals, and in plants; the size of the individual virus ranges from 10 to 300 mμ. They cannot be visualized with the light microscope; their morphological characteristics have been investigated by means of electron microscopy. Chemically, they consist of nucleic acid and protein. The elementary bodies of the infected cells are the carriers of infectiosity. Viruses producing pathologic skin changes primarily in men are those causing molluscum contagiosum, verrucae, condyloma acuminatum, herpes simplex, zoster, varicellae, variola vera, vaccinia, milker's nodules, foot and mouth disease, cat scratch disease, various exanthematous infectious diseases, and lymphogranuloma venereum (Nicolas-Favre). Viruses are cultivated most successfully when inoculated into chicken eggs.

Molluscum Contagiosum (Bateman)

After an incubation period of 2 weeks to several months, discrete pinhead-sized, slowly growing, umbilicated, globular papules develop predominantly on the face (cheeks, eyelids and forehead), neck, and external genitals and surrounding areas of children. They may become inflamed and grow to pea-size or larger (Fig. 107). Dense crops may form reddish-brown, verrucous lesions, with the central depression still visible. When compressed laterally, the eruptions discharge a cheesy white granular core through their central depressions. Mollusca involving the eyelids occasionally reach considerable size. They may cause stubborn conjunctivitis.

Warts

Verruca vulgaris, verruca plana juvenilis, verruca plantaris, and condyloma acuminatum are contagious, virus-induced tumors. The contagiositiy of warts was recognized as early as 1896 (Jadassohn). Incubation periods range from 4 weeks to 20 months. The same type of virus has been isolated from the morphologically widely differing lesions mentioned above. The clinical appearance of the verrucous tumors seems to be determined by the site on which they grow.

Verrucae Planae Juveniles
(Flat Warts)

Flat, polygonal, skin-colored or slightly yellowish to reddish-brown papules develop on the dorsal aspects of fingers and hands, on the distal portions of the forearms, and in the face (Fig. 108). Flat warts are seen predominantly in children and young adults. They appear suddenly and in great numbers, are often persistent, but may disappear just as suddenly and spontaneously. This is probably the reason they sometimes respond well to hypnosis.

Verrucae Vulgares

These differ from flat warts by their size, their rough horny surface, and their predilection for the hands (Fig. 109). *Periungual* and *plantar warts* are especially troublesome. On the eyelids, in the beard area, and on the lips, the verrucae develop as threadlike tumors and are therefore referred to as *filiform warts*.

Condylomata Acuminata
(Venereal Warts)

Multiple soft, moist, reddish or skin-colored, pedunculated, small papillary tumors, often coalescing into large tumors with cauliflowerlike surface (Fig. 110), may involve the entire genital or anal region. They grow primarily on moist, macerated skin (vaginal discharge, phimosis, balanitis) and are sometimes venereal in origin.

Epidermodysplasia Verruciformis (Lewandowsky-Lutz)

This disorder shows numerous verrucous lesions of different morphology, particularly on the dorsa of the hands and feet, on the face, and on the neck. Positive inoculation experiments suggest that it is a generalized verucosis, not a different disease entity. Some authors believe it to be an autosomal recessive precancerous genodermatosis.

Herpes Simplex

This eruption, which is preceded by mild itching or burning, consists of grouped vesicles of uniform size on an erythematous base, involving the skin and mucous membranes. According to its localization, herpes is denoted as *herpes facialis*, *labialis*, (Figs. 111 and

112), *progenitalis,* or *digitalis* (*herpetic "whithlow"*). When the vesicles break, small superficial ulcers form on the skin and mucous membranes. Recurrent episodes are typical of herpes simplex. Regular recurrences at the same site are called herpes recidivans in loco (Fig. 113). The causative organism, a virus, can be inoculated into the rabbit cornea, producing a punctate keratitis. Two different antigenic strains have been isolated. Herpes virus hominis, type 1, commonly affects the skin and mucosa of the mouth. Type 2 primarily infects the mucosa of the genitalia and neighboring skin. A relationship between type 2 and cervical cancer is presently discussed. A smear from the base of the vesicle (Tzanck test) shows multinucleated giant cells. Outbreak of the disease appears to be dependent on certain precipitating factors, such as menstruation, traumatization, sunlight exposure, gastrointestinal upsets, and psychological influences. Herpes simplex may also occur, in the form of typical *fever blisters* or *cold sores,* associated with febrile disorders. These different herpetic infections develop in patients with antibodies who were exposed the to virus before. Typical primary forms of herpes in patients without antibodies are *acute primary herpetic gingivostomatitis,* clinically presenting as *aphthous stomatitis, acute herpetic vulvovaginitis* and *acute herpetic keratoconjunctivitis.* They are usually seen in children. Transmission of the infection may be exogenous or hematogenous. The incubation period is 2 to 5 days.

Eczema Herpeticum

This disease is also known as Kaposi's varicelliform eruption. It is a grave complication of eczematous eruptions, particularly of atopic dermatitis. It is characterized by numerous vesicles and pustules of uniform size superimposed on the preexisting dermatosis (Fig. 114), involvement of the oral mucosa, and dendritic keratitis. The disease is fetal in 10 per cent of adult patients and in 20 per cent of infants.

Zoster (Shingles)

Shingles are caused by herpesvirus varicellae. Zoster is a unilateral, often band-like vesicular eruption on an erythemato-edematous base, situated along the distribution of nerves from one or several posterior ganglia (Figs. 115—117). The disease produces immunity.

The grouped vesicular lesions later become purulent and umbilicated. *Hemorrhagic zoster* is characterized by hemorrhagic vesicles; *necrotic* or *gangrenous zoster* by necrotic degeneration of the base of the vesicles. Severe, burning neuritic pain may precede, accompany, or follow the outbreak of shingles, especially in older patients. Sensory impairment and transient muscle paresis may occur. The cerebrospinal fluid often shows increase in protein content and cell count.

A smear from the base of the lesions shows multinucleated giant cells. The disease may occur as a complication of leukemia (Fig. 118). Hodgkin's disease, internal cancer, administration of arsenicals, or carbon monoxide poisoning. Zoster is considered an infection with Herpesvirus varicellae in a partially immune host.

Varicella

(Chickenpox)

In this febrile disease, pink macules develop into papules and then into pinhead- to lentil-sized, clear, tense, sometimes umbilicated vesicles on an erythematous base. They become purulent and eventually dry out with crust formation. The first lesions appear on face and back; later the eruption becomes generalized. New crops of vesicles may appear repeatedly, associated with elevated temperatures. Simultaneous existence of various developmental stages of varicella (macules, papules, vesicles, pustules, crusts) and involvement of the oral mucosa (especially the hard palate) are characteristic features. Varicella usually affects children, but adults also may contract the disease, which produces immunity. The Tzanck test shows multinucleated giant cells. Both zoster and varicella are caused by the same virus, Herpes virus varicellae.

Variola Vera

(Smallpox)

The initial stage of this infection, following an incubation period of 8 to 12 days, is characterized by a 3-day period of fever, severe headache, backache, and vomiting. In most cases, a transient macular rash appears on the face and arms. The fever subsides after 3 days. Starting on the fifth day approximately, the exanthem is transformed into firm papules, then into vesicles, and finally into the typical umbilicated pustules on an erythematous base (suppurative stage) (Fig. 119); simultaneously, the temperature rises again. This stage is completed on or about the eighth day. The exanthem is generalized, with special emphasis on the face, arms, and palms. Particularly dense aggregates are seen in the vicinity of scar tissue or pressure areas. The oral mucosa shows ulcerating vesicles. On the twelfth day, the pustules begin to dry. The crusts are shed after 1 to 1½ weeks, and scars remain. In the presence of hemorrhagic pustules or coalescing lesions (variola confluens), the prognosis is grave. Characteristically, all lesions of variola vera are in the same stage of development simultaneously.

Vaccinia

Prophylaxis against smallpox is based on vaccination with vaccinia lymph. Jenner originally used cowpox lymph (1796). Both viruses are closely related but not identical.

Dermatologically important complications of smallpox vaccination are *accidental vaccination* (autoinoculation of other areas of the body), *inoculation vaccinia* (transmission to noninoculated persons) (Fig. 120), and *eczema vaccinatum*.

Eczema Vaccinatum

This disease is caused by inoculation of the vaccinia virus into skin altered by preexisting eczematous conditions, particularly atopic dermatitis. This complication, as well as eczema herpeticum, was included in the older term "Kaposi's varicelliform eruption". After an incubation period of 5 to 12 days, the disease runs a predictable febrile course, regardless of the site of infection. From the face, where the changes are most marked (Fig. 121), multiple umbilicated pustules spread centrifugally over the entire integument, sometimes healing with cicatrization.

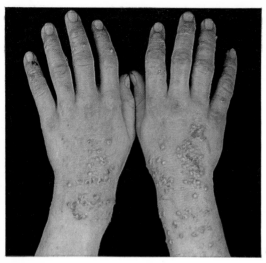

63

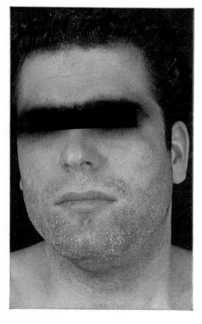

63 Follicular impetigo (Bock-hart). Superficial ostiofolliculitis confined to the hair follicles. Each of the centrally depressed lesions is pierced by a hair.

64 Sycosis (folliculitis) barbae. Beard area studded with small follicular erythematous pustules.

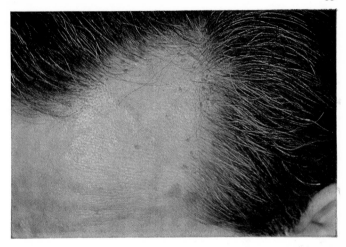

65 Acne necroticans (acne varioliformis). Recurrent, discrete, red papules and pustules healing with small depressed scars.

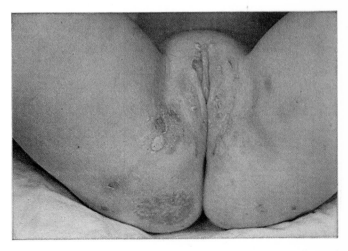

66 Bullous impetigo. In a 5-year-old girl. Large purulent bullae and pustules.

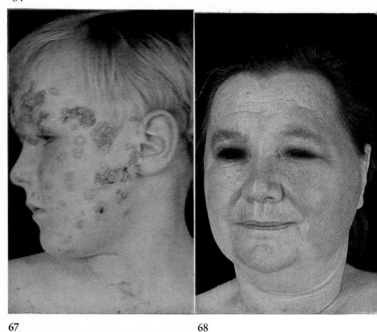

67   68

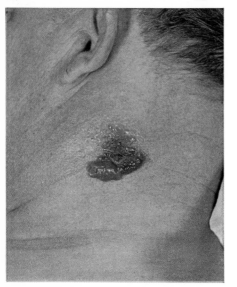

67 Impetigo contagiosa. New lesions covered wi heavy, stuck-on, grayis brown and honey-color crusts; caused by strept cocci. Older healing lesio

68 Erysipelas. Sharply c cumscribed, tender, hot, re edematous area with advar ing raised border.

69 Anthrax (malignant pu tule). Formation of a bla eschar over the drying hem orrhagic bulla with infiltr tion of the surrounding t sue.

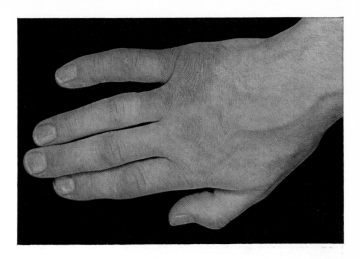

70 Erysipeloid (Rosenbach). Well defined, violaceous-red, edematous infiltration with arciform advancing border.

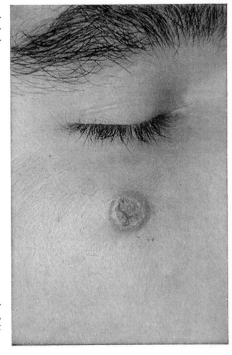

71 Cutaneous leishmaniasis. Isolated, crateriform, ulcerating nodule on right cheek.

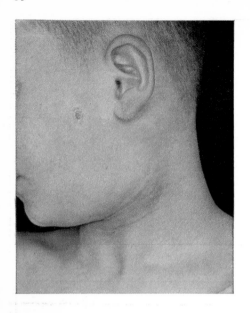

72 Primary inoculation tuberculosis. Tuberculous primary complex. Indurated ulcer with prominent lymphadenopathy in a young boy.

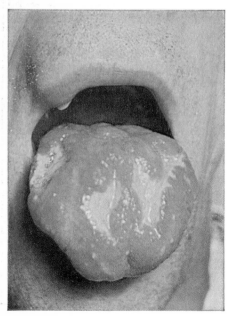

73 Tuberculosis cutis orificialis. Rapidly ulcerating indolent lesions of the tongue.

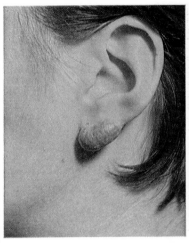

74

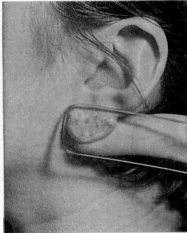

75

74 and **75** **Lupus vulgaris.**
Diascopic examination re-
veals multiple, small, nodular
infiltrations of apple-jelly col-
or.

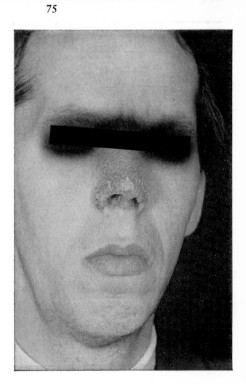

76 **Lupus vulgaris.** Erythema, infiltration, and scaling of
the nose.

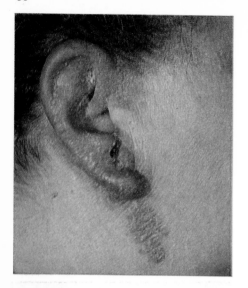

77 Lupus vulgaris. Ear, spreading to periauricular skin.

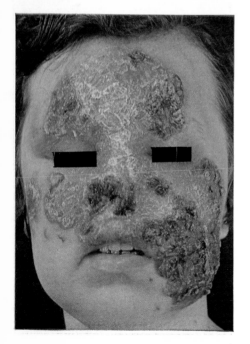

78, 79 and **80 Lupus vulgaris.** Widespread lesions of the face with heavy crusts and ulceration before, during, and after INH therapy. Typical "worn-off" appearance of nose.

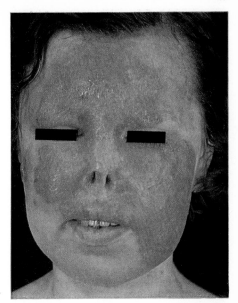

79

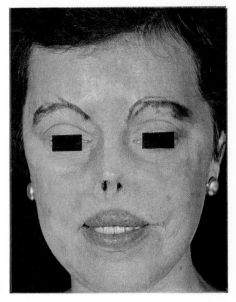

80

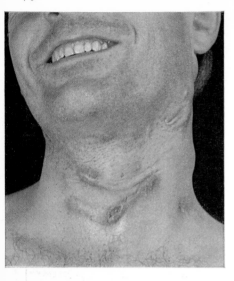

81 Scrofuloderma. Ulcerating lymph nodes with fistulous openings healing with hypertrophic scars.

82 Tuberculosis verrucosa cutis. Crusted verrucous plaque on dorsum of the hand.

83 Lichen scrofulosorum. Disseminated patches of firm lichenoid papules.

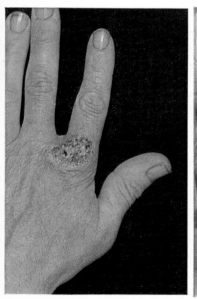

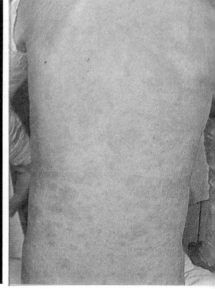

82

83

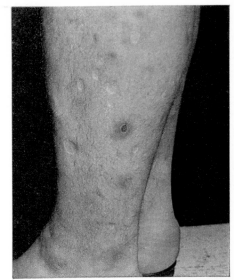

84 Papulonecrotic tuberculid.
Most lesions have healed with typical, varioliform, depressed scars.

85 Erythema induratum (Bazin). Nodular discolored lesions of the calves with ulceration and scarring.

86 Lupus miliaris disseminatus faciei. Symmetrical, small, soft, reddish-brown nodules of the face.

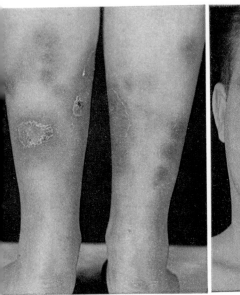

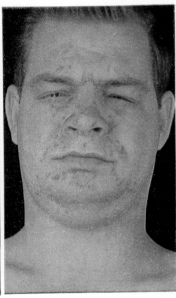

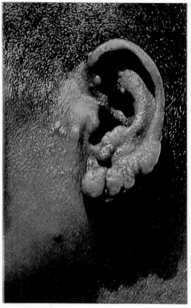

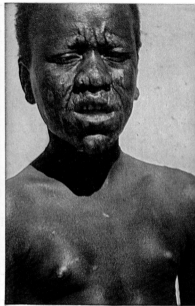

87 Lepromatous leprosy. Nodular infiltration of the ear lobe, a commonly involved area.

88 Lepromatous leprosy. Nodular infiltration of the face, partial loss of the eyebrows and eyelashes; gynecomastia due to endocrine changes following lepromatous infiltration of the testes.

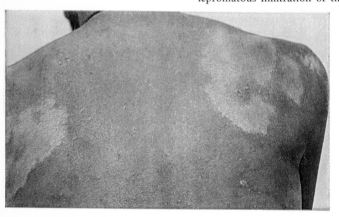

89 Tuberculoid leprosy. Sharply outlined, slightly raised, anesthetic, depigmented lesions with central clearing.

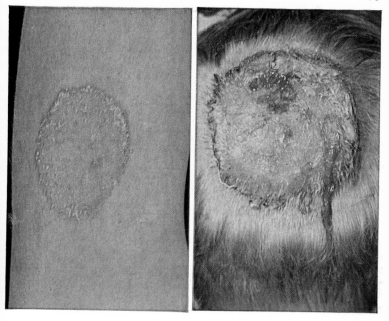

90 Tinea corporis. Oval lesion with erythema, vesiculation, and scaling, particularly of the border of the lesion.

91 Kerion of the scalp. Well defined, soft, succulent lesion with partial hair loss and purulent discharge.

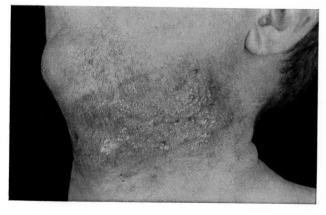

92 Tinea barbae (sycosis barbae). Elevated, soft, purulent nodular lesions with irregular surface.

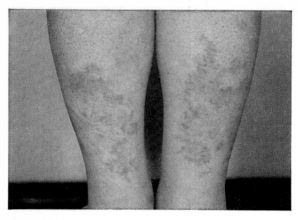

93 Follicular dermatophytosis. Deep pruritic nodules of the lower legs.

94 Tinea unguium (onychomycosis). Dirty yellowish-gray discoloration and brittleness of nail plate, usually beginning at the lateral or distal portion of the nail.

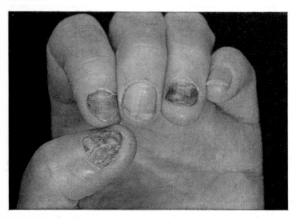

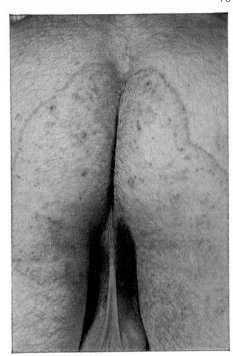

95 Tinea cruris et inguinalis. Sharply defined, eruption with raised, erythemato-vesicular border in adjacent gluteal region.

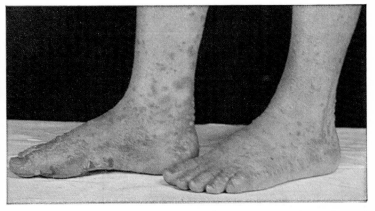

96 Tinea pedis, dyshidrotic variety. With small, red, maculopapular and vesicular lesions.

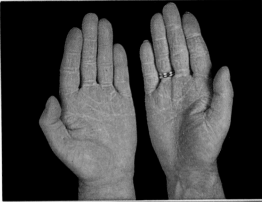

97 Tinea man-
uum, squamous
hyperkeratotic
variety. Often
due to trichophy-
ton rubrum.

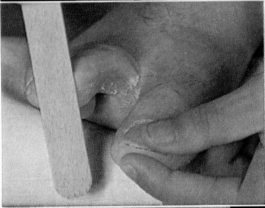

98 Tinea pedis,
intertriginous
variety. With ery-
thema, scaling,
maceration, and
fissures of inter-
digital area.

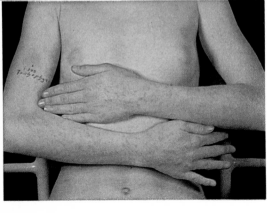

99 Dermato-
phytid of the
hands and arms.
Positive tricho-
phytin reaction.

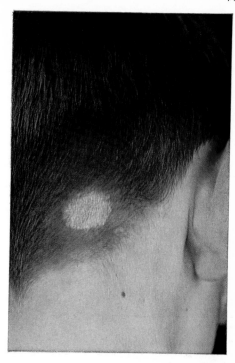

100 Tinea capitis.
Sharply marginated round patch with whitish pityriasiform scaling and short broken-off hairs.

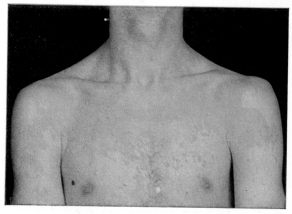

101 Tinea versicolor. Yellowish-brown, confluent lesions with pityriasiform scaling.

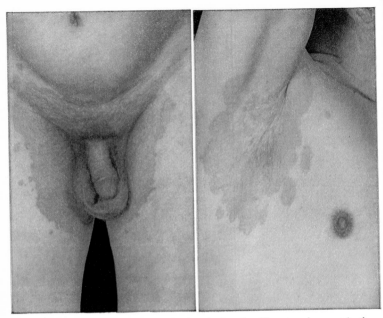

102 and 103 Erythrasma. Extensive inguinal and axillary involvement in the same patient. The lesions show coral red fluorescence under Wood's light.

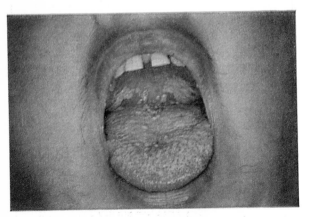

104 Thrush (moniliasis of the oral cavity). Erythema, edema, and whitish coating of mucous membranes.

79

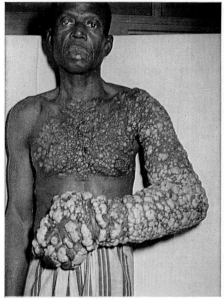

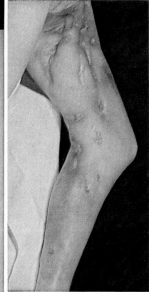

105 Chromoblastomycosis. Brownish and whitish verrucous and papillomatous lesions on the left arm and trunk.

106 Primary actinomycosis of the skin. Hard tender infiltration with sinus tracts and purulent discharge.

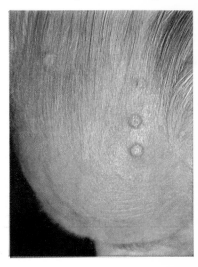

107 Mollusca contagiosa of the scalp. Discrete, globular, umbilicated nontender nodules of varying size.

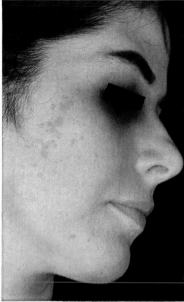 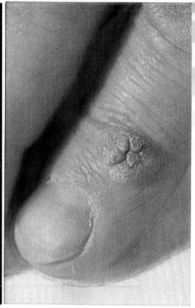

108 Verrucae planae juveniles.
Discrete and coalescent reddish-brown flat polygonal papules.

109 Verruca vulgaris. Typical hard,
raised, verrucous tumor with irregular horny surface.

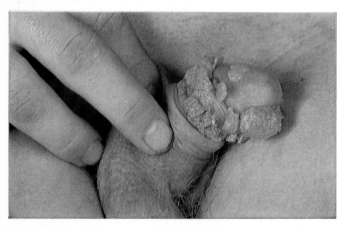

110 Condylomata acuminata. Typical cauliflower-like, soft, moist,
reddish papillary tumors on the prepuce, in the coronary sulcus, and
on the glans penis.

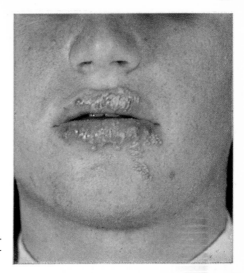

111 Herpes simplex. Elicited by excessive sun irradiation (herpes solaris).

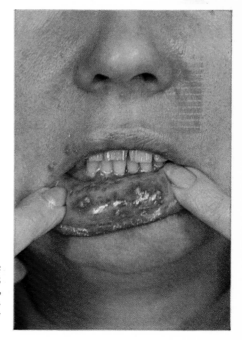

112 Herpes simplex. Some vesicles are still intact; others have become eroded, giving rise to small ulcers. Caused by Herpesvirus hominis, type 1.

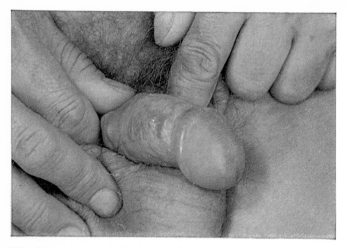

113 Herpes progenitalis. In this location, herpes simplex lesions erode rapidly; consequently, only flat erosions are seen. Herpes of the genital area is usually caused by Herpesvirus hominis, type 2.

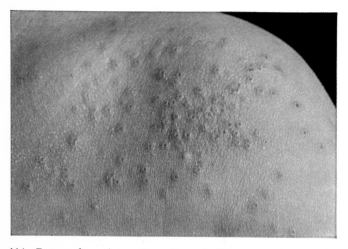

114 Eczema herpeticum. Kaposi's varicelliform eruption on the shoulder of an atopic patient. Characteristic discrete umbilicated herpes simplex lesions.

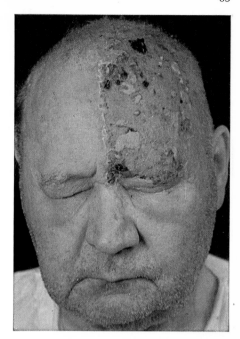

115 Gangrenous zoster.
Following the ophthalmic nerve, involving skin of the forehead, scalp, upper eyelid, and upper portion of the nose.

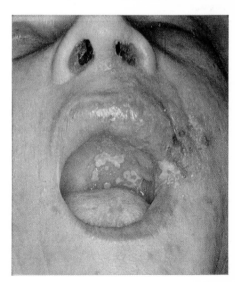

116 Zoster. Grouped vesicles following the distribution of the maxillary nerve, involving skin of the left cheek, the upper lip, and the oral and nasal mucosa. Skin and mucous membrane lesions are often preceded by severe toothache.

84

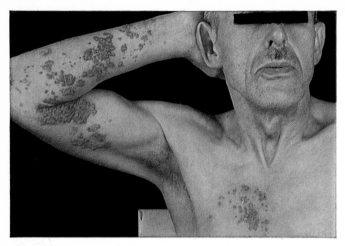

117 Zoster. Typical herpetic, grouped, hemorrhagic vesicles and pustules extending from C 6 to T 2.

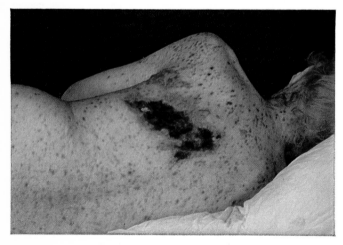

118 Generalized zoster. Associated with chronic lymphatic leukemia. Deep necroses in the thoracic segments 4 and 5.

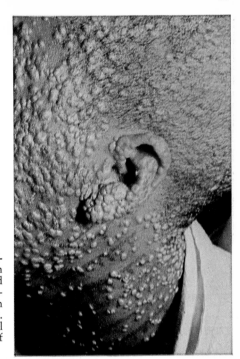

119 Variola vera (small-pox). Generalized eruption with typical umbilicated pustules on an erythematous base associated with severe systemic symptoms. In contrast to varicella, all lesions are in same stage of development.

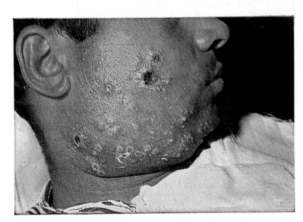

120 Inoculation vaccinia. Umbilicated and necrotic pustules in a patient who had never been vaccinated.

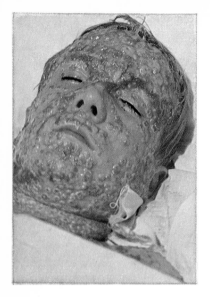

121 Eczema vaccinatum. Typical coalescing umbilicated pustules superimposed on atopic dermatitis (Kaposi's varicelliform eruption).

Sarcoidosis, Melkersson-Rosenthal Syndrome, Granuloma Annulare

Sarcoidosis (Besnier-Boeck-Schaumann)

Besnier (1889) described lupus pernio; Boeck (1899), multiple lesions of benign sarcoidosis of the skin. In 1904, Kreibich reported several cases of lupus pernio with multiple lesions on other parts of the integument, and fusiform swelling of the fingers with cystic radiolucent defects of the phalanges. The term, *ostitis fibrosa multiplex cystica* was first used by Jüngling (1919) to describe these osseous changes. Schaumann was one of the first to recognize the characteristic pulmonary changes which resemble miliary tuberculosis.

Histologically, sarcoidosis is characterized by a tuberculoid reaction with epitheliod cells. In the United States, a large percentage of the patients are negroes. It is a disease of adults and is more common in females. The *superficial disseminated form* of Besnier-Boeck-Schaumann disease, also known as benign miliary lupoid, presents pinhead- to pea-sized maculopapular or lichenoid isolated skin lesions of reddish-brown to livid coloring. Diascopy reveals yellowish-brownish punctate infiltrations. Occasionally, the nodules coalesce into serpiginous or annular lesions.

The *nodular form* of the disease is characterized by separate, brownish to bluish-red, indurated nodules which could be as large as a walnut (Fig. 122). Subcutaneous nodules of the lower legs are known as the Darier-Roussy type of sarcoidosis. When the nodules show a more purple coloring resembling frostbite (pernio), they are referred to as lupus pernio (Fig. 123). The systemic nature of sarcoidosis is emphasized by such findings as hilar lymphadenopathy, miliary pulmonary infiltrations, ostitis multiplex cystica and fusiform swelling of the phalanges (Fig. 124), Heerfordt syndrome (uveoparotic fever), Mikulicz syndrome (involvement of lacrimal and salivary glands), and involvement of lymph nodes, liver, or other internal organs. Total serum protein is usually elevated (increase in gamma globulins). Hypercalcemia is a frequent finding. Some authors consider sarcoidosis an atypical form of tuberculosis; the tuberculin skin test is negative. Others believe the disease to be a syndrome that may have a variety of causes.

Melkersson-Rosenthal Syndrome

This syndrome is characterized by recurring edema of the lips and upper face, facial paralysis or paresis, and scrotal tongue (Figs. 125 and 126). Systemic symptoms are absent. Tuberculosis and allergic processes have been discussed as etiologic factors.

88

Granuloma Annulare (Radcliffe-Crocker)

This disease has a predilection for the extensor surfaces of the fingers, the dorsa of the hands, the external ear, and the dorsa of the feet; occasionally, disseminated eruptions are seen. The lesions are small, nontender, sharply defined, deep-seated, firm papules or nodules which are skin-colored, whitish or slightly erythematous. They spread centrifugally, forming annular configurations with normal-appearing centers (Fig. 127). The disease is easily diagnosed and has a favorable prognosis. It is common in children and young adults; rarely, tuberculosis may be found to be an etiologic factor. In some cases, a rheumatic hyperergic reaction may be present.

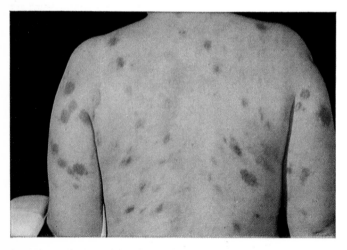

122 Sarcoidosis, nodular type. Bluish-red, firm nodules in the face, on the trunk, and on the extremities. Yellowish-brownish punctate infiltrations are seen under diascopic examination.

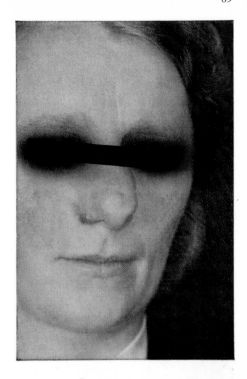

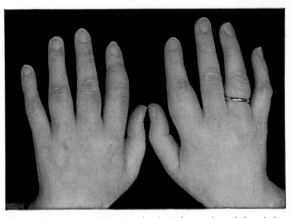

123 and **124 Sarcoidosis.** Bluish indurated nodule of the nose (lupus pernio) and fusiform swelling of the fingers due to ostitis multiplex cystica.

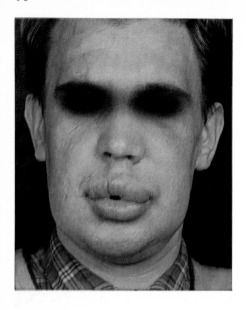

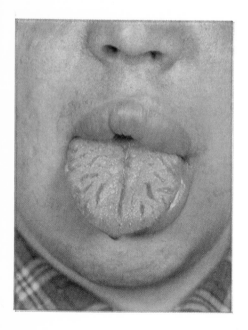

125 and 126 Melkersson-Rosenthal syndrome. Recurrent edema of the lips, left facial paresis, and scrotal tongue.

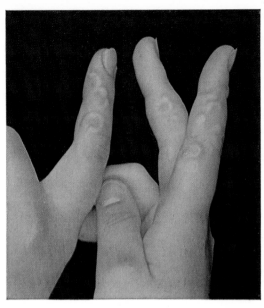

127 Granuloma annulare. Solitary, annular, and arciform indurated skin lesions.

Zoonotic Dermatoses

Pediculosis Capitis

Infestation with the head louse (Pediculus capitis), which is smaller and more slender than the body louse (Pediculus corporis), is usually due to poor scalp hygiene. Its eggs (nits) are glued in long rows to the scalp hair, usually beginning at the temporal aspects; frequently, however, the entire scalp is involved. The infestation causes itching, and the resulting scratching leads to secondary changes of the scalp with oozing and impetiginization. The hair may become matted. Whereas a severe case of pediculosis is easily diagnosed, it may be difficult to detect live lice on a fairly well groomed scalp. A useful diagnostic point is the fact that dandruff is easily removed from the hair, while nits are firmly attached.

Pediculosis Corporis

The mobile body louse is found on skin areas covered by clothing. Its eggs (nits), shiny, transparent, ovoid, inconspicuous structures, often of the same color as their background, are deposited on fibers and seams of clothing. Newly hatched lice are so small that they can be visualized only with a lens. Once one member of a household is affected, the infestation usually spreads rapidly to other members. Since the parasites also invade furniture and blankets, disinfection of every room and all clothing is indicated.

Pediculosis Pubis

The pubic louse (Phthirus pubis), of greater width than length, has strong claw-like extremities which firmly grip the infested hair. The parasite is flat, pale gray, and readily detected when in motion, but easily mistaken for a small crust when immobile. The infestation usually begins in the pubic area, then spreads along the trunk to the axillary hair. Occasionally pubic lice may be found in the ciliary and superciliary hair of adults, where they may cause conjunctivitis, and on the scalps of children. A secretion transmitted by their bites produces pigmented steel gray-blue spots, so-called "tâches bleues" (maculae caeruleae). The nits, deposited on the hair, are provided with a coverlet which remains open after the lice have hatched. Excoriations are usually absent because patients suffering from pediculosis pubis tend to "rub" rather than scratch.

Scabies

Scabies is caused by a mite, Acarus or Sarcoptes scabiei. The female deposits her eggs in burrows deep in the horny layer of the skin. In addition to eggs, these tunnels contain fecal and other matter. The larvae hatch after 2½ to 3 days and reach sexual maturity within 2 to 3 weeks. The males stay on the surface of the skin, usually in skin folds, and die after copulation. Sites of predilection are the soft parts of the skin, particularly the interdigital spaces of the fingers; in young children, the palms and soles also may be involved. In adult males, the external genitals are not infrequently affected (Fig. 128), and in females the nipple area may be involved. The burrows may be straight, angular, or curved, and have a slightly raised, vesicular, erythematous area at their terminal point. Subsequently, papules and vesicles covered with crusts develop on the wrists, in the antecubital areas, and in the anterior axillary folds, less frequently on the legs, back, neck, and face. Various degrees of excoriations are seen, depending on the severity of the pruritus. In chronic cases, impetiginization and eczematization may occur. The diagnosis is established by demonstration of the burrows and of the parasites in potassium hydroxide preparations.

Animal mites that may be transferred to man temporarily are Dermanyssus avium, Acarus equi, Acarus cani, Acarus cati, and mites living in foodstuffs, cereals (grain itch), and straw, such as Pediculoides ventricosus. Their bite induces papules and similar reactions, thus producing a scabies-like clinical picture. However, these mites do not dig burrows in the skin, but live on the skin surface for short periods of time; they may be visualized with a lens.

Tick Bites

Pruritic nodules, papules, or urticarial reactions can be caused by tick bites. Ticks occur in woody and scrubby territory, and penetrate into the skin of man and animals upon contact. Engorged with blood, the parasite becomes a bean-sized, spherical or pear-shaped, bluish-black structure. A common method of removing the ticks is by touching it with oil, glycerin, gasoline, or a lighted cigarette; usually, however, the head is torn off during this manipulation, and causes local inflammation of the skin. Ticks are also important as vectors of infectious diseases.

Pulicosis
(Flea Bites)

The human flea (Pulex irritans), a wingless insect 2 to 4 mm. in length, has become quite rare. Through its bite, a hyperemia-producing and coagulation-inhibiting secretion is injected into the tissue; the human skin reacts to this irritant by forming wheals and papules with characteristic tiny hemorrhagic puncta in the center. Vesicular reactions, secondary infections, and even purpura pulicosa have been encountered.

Culicosis
(Mosquito Bites)

Flies are a common pest, especially near stagnant waters. Their bites produce wheals with central puncta, or — especially in children — bullous reactions (Fig. 129). *Papular urticaria* (strophulus infantum) is in most cases due to hypersensitivity to flea, bedbug, and other insect bites. It is a common diesase of children between 2 and 7 years of age and occurs during the summer months. It consists of numerous papules, urticarial lesions, and excoriations, particularly in exposed skin areas.

Creeping Eruption
(Larva Migrans)

The typical migratory, tortuous, threadlike, urticarial lesions correspond to the burrowing of different larvae in tropical climates. The most common types are caused by various larvae of Ancylostoma (helminthiasis) or botflies (myiasis).

Filariasis

Pathologic changes produced by various filariae in the human organism are lymphangitis, lymphadenopathy, and obstruction of the lymph vessels resulting in elephantiasis of the genitals (Fig. 130) and lower extremities (Wuchereria bancrofti), cutaneous nodules (Onchocerca volvulus), ulcerations and inflammatory skin changes on the feet and lower legs (Dracunculus medinensis) (Fig. 131), and transient allergic reaction of the skin (Loa loa). The filarial parasites are nematodes found in the tropics; they are transmitted by various species of Culex, Cinopheles, and Aedes, and produce microfilariae which require suitable hosts for their development.

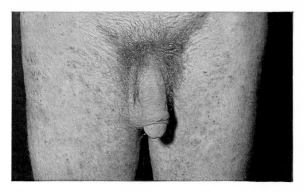

128 Scabies. Inflamed burrows in widespread papulo-vesicular lesions of the thighs with many excoriations and punctate hemorrhagic crusts.

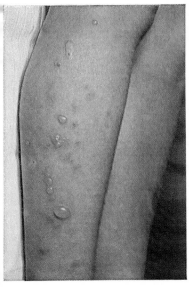

129 Papular urticaria (strophulus). Papular, urticarial, and bullous reaction due to mosquito bites.

130 Filariasis. Unusually large elephantiasis of the scrotum.

96

131 Dracunculus medinensis. The parasite extracted from the leg is fastened with a string tied around the leg. The extracted, somewhat dehydrated portion of the parasite is seen pointing toward the right.

Hereditary Cutaneous Disorders

This group comprises skin diseases widely differing in their symptomatology, but united by the fact that they are inheritable.

Ichthyosiform and Keratotic Genodermatoses

Ichthyosis Vulgaris
(Ichthyosis Simplex)

This is the most common ichthyotic disorder. It is inherited as a simple autosomal dominant of variable expressivity. One of the parents is often affected. Scaling is usually absent at birth, and develops during the first years of life. Follicular hyperkeratosis on the lateral surfaces of the extremities is an early manifestation of the disease. Atopic disorders are often associated with ichthyosis vulgaris. Scaling involves many areas, but usually spares the flexural creases (Fig. 132). On the trunk, the scales are small and flaky and fixed at one end; over the legs the scales are large. Many patients with ichthyosis vulgaris show an accentuation of palmar and plantar markings. Microscopic findings include a thin epidermis; the granular layer is reduced or absent.

X-linked Ichthyosis

This rare disorder is inherited as an x-linked trait and primarily affects males, the sons of female heterozygotes or "carriers". Scaling develops in early infancy and involves neck, trunk, buttocks and extremities. The palms and soles appear normal, Slit-lamp examination of the cornea often reveals opacities of the posterior capsule or Descemet's membrane. Epidermal cell kinetics are within normal limits.

Lamellar Ichthyosis

This severe autosomal recessive disease was originally considered a variant of ichthyosis vulgaris or as the dry form of congenital ichthyosiform erythroderma. Usually neither parent is affected. Scaling is apparent at birth, and even in later years almost the entire surface is involved. Face, palms, and soles demonstrate considerable hyperkeratosis, but no noticeable scaling. Most other areas show large coarse scales adherent in their centers with slightly raised edges. Studies of epidermal cell proliferation kinetics show an increased cell transit rate through the epidermis and an increased rate of stratum corneum formation. Microscopic examination shows marked hyperkeratosis with a prominent granular layer and many mitotic figures.

Epidermolytic Hyperkeratosis

This rare genodermatosis was originally classified as the bullous type of congenital ichthyosiform erythroderma (Brocq) or ichthyosis hystrix. It is inherited as an autosomal dominant trait; other members of the family are often affected. Epidermolytic hyperkeratosis is present at birth, and may form vesicular and bullous lesions (Fig. 133). Characteristic thick, gray-brown, often verruciform scales involve most of the body, particularly the flexural creases. Bacterial infections are common. As in lamellar ichthyosis, the cell transit rate through the epidermis is markedly increased. Histologic examination reveals extreme hyperkeratosis and dense collections of keratohyaline-like granules in the granular layer. Many large vacuolated cells are seen in the Malpighian layer.

Pachyonychia Congenita (Jadassohn-Lewandowsky)
(Keratosis Multiformis Idiopathica)
(Siemens)

Changes of the nails and multiple anomalies of keratinization of the skin and mucous membranes are usually present at birth. The nail plates are thickened and firmly attached. Keratotic follicular lesions (keratosis pilaris) are seen on the extensor surfaces of the extremities. Occasionally, hyperhidrosis, abnormalities of hair, teeth, and bone development, bulla formation, and mental deficiency are observed. The pattern of inheritance is unknown. Familial incidence with strong sex limitation to males has been reported.

Keratoma Palmare et Plantare Hereditarium (Unna-Thost)
(Keratosis Palmaris et Plantaris)

The affected areas, usually the palms and soles, are covered with a yellowish horny layer of even thickness (Fig. 134 and 135). The disease is inherited as a dominant, it usually manifests itself during the first 2 years of life. A 1 cm. red border separates the keratoma from the surrounding normal skin.

Mal de Meleda
(Keratosis Palmaris et Plantaris)
(Siemens)

This is a diffuse symmetrical keratoderma, usually beginning on the palms and soles. It progressively involves the dorsa of fingers, hands, toes, forearms and lower legs. The disease is transmitted as a recessive characteristic. Greither described a dominant form under the name of *keratosis extremitatum hereditaria progrediens*.

Keratoma Palmare et Plantare Dissipatum Hereditarium (Brauer)

The punctate, cone-shaped, horny lesions seen in shallow depressions of the skin on the palms and soles usually occur at the beginning of the third decade of life. The horny plugs may be shed, leaving pit-like scars (Fig. 136 and 137). The disease is inherited as a dominant condition.

Arsenical keratoses also present as punctate palmar lesions.

Keratosis Follicularis (Darier)

The primary lesions (Figs. 138—140) are small firm papules developing in follicular orifices or on normal skin. Each lesion is covered by a yellowish-brown crust; the base is sometimes erythematous (Fig. 138). The papules have a tendency to coalesce and develop into papillomatous, dirty and greasy patches. Areas of predilection are the chest, back (Fig. 140), sacral area, scalp, face, dorsa of the hands, and body folds. Decomposition of the horny masses results in exudation, irritation, and an unpleasant odor, especially in creases and folds of the skin where maceration develops easily. Irregularly shaped papillomatous growths may develop underneath the keratotic masses. "Formes frustes" are characterized by lesions on the back of the hands reminiscent of flat warts. The oral mucous membranes may show flat nodules and irregular papillary lesions (Fig. 139).

The disease may have its onset in the first year of life, usually later. In all cases, even in mild forms, characteristic interruptions of the dermatoglyphics of the palms can be observed.

Inheritance of the disorder is of the autosomal irregular dominant type.

Keratosis Pilaris

(Lichen Pilaris, Keratosis Suprafollicularis)

This is a very common abnormality, presenting as discrete conical hyperkeratoses of the follicular orifices. The corneous plugs often enclose fine lanugo hairs. The lesions are seen predominantly in adolescents, on the extensor aspects of the extremities, and in the gluteal area. Patients with ichthyosis vulgaris often show similar changes.

Other Genodermatoses

Adenoma Sebaceum (Pringle)

(Epiloia, Tuberous Sclerosis)

This disease, inherited as a dominant condition, is quite variable in its symptomatology. It usually manifests itself in the first decade, but becomes more prominent during pubescence. The most common symptom combination occurs in the form of a triad consisting of mental deficiency, epilepsy, and various skin tumors. Among these are organic sebaceous gland nevi (the term "adenoma sebaceum" is a misnomer) in the form of multiple, rounded, firm, skin-colored or red papules or nodules in the central portion of the face (Fig. 141), often associated with telangiectases, peri- and subungual fibromas on the toes and fingers (Koenen's tumors) (Fig. 142), verrucous pigmented nevi on the trunk, and pinhead-sized papillomatous nodules on the oral mucosa, especially the gingiva. Tumors of the retina (phacomas), brain tumors (gliomas), and atypical mixed tumors of internal organs are also seen. The disease is probably related to neurofibromatosis.

Neurofibromatosis (von Recklinghausen)

This systemic disease, transmitted as an irregular dominant condition, originates from immature nerve cells or Schwann cells. Typical symptoms of neurofibromatosis are numerous oval, brownish-yellow "café au lait" spots, with a relatively smooth border, on the trunk and extremities (more than six are considered diagnostic); pigmented nevi or freckles; vascular nevi; soft rounded or pendulous skin-colored neurofibromas (Fig. 143); neurinomas; elephantiasic tissue accumulations (dermatolysis) (Fig. 144); tumors of the spinal nerves and the spinal canal; intracranial tumors; neurofibromas of internal organs; skeletal abnormalities; retinal tumors (phacomas); hypertrichosis of the sacral region; endocrine disturbances; mental deficiency; and psychic alterations. Abortive oligosymptomatic forms are seen occasionally.

Pseudoxanthoma Elasticum (Darier)

This anomaly is most commonly seen in female adults as asymptomatic yellowish to orange-colored papules in linear distribution or leathery plaques, particularly on neck (Fig. 145), axillae, face, and groin. Histologically, the changes are limited to the elastic fibers (elastorrhexis) In addition to the skin, elastic changes occur in the fundus of the eye (angioid streaks) leading to impaired vision (Grönblad-Strandberg syndrome), in the cardiovascular system (angina pectoris, hypertension, intermittent claudication, gastrointestinal hemorrhages). The disorder is inherited primarily as an autotomal recessive, rarely as an autosomal dominant characteristic.

Cutis Hyperelastica (Ehlers-Danlos)

This rare dystrophic anomaly is characterized by cutaneous hyperextensibility (Fig. 146), extreme fragility of the skin and of the blood vessels resulting in hematomas and atrophic changes in areas of frequent trauma (Fig. 147), and hyperflexibility of the joints. It is inherited as a dominant trait, but may occur in the absence of demonstrable genetic factors. Blue sclerae, epicanthal folds, and aortic aneurysms are common in this condition.

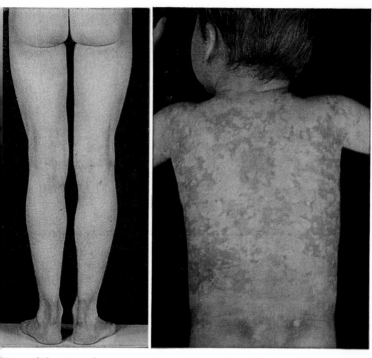

132 Ichthyosis vulgaris. Symmetrical involvement of both legs with exception of the popliteal areas.

133 Epidermolytic hyperkeratosis (Congenital ichthyosiform erythroderma, bullous type). Hyperkeratotic areas with erythema, bullae and scaling.

Peutz-Jeghers syndrome, xeroderma pigmentosum, hydroa vacciniforme, familial idiopathic hypercholesteremic xanthomatosis, gout, and *Hartnup syndrome* are other genodermatoses which are discussed elsewhere.

Bullous Genodermatoses

Epidermolysis Bullosa Simplex

In this abnormality, which is transmitted as a dominant mendelian trait and has a higher incidence in the male sex, minor mechanical trauma induces bullae on exposed areas of the body, particularly on the feet (Fig. 148), hands, elbows, and knees. The lesions heal without scarring.

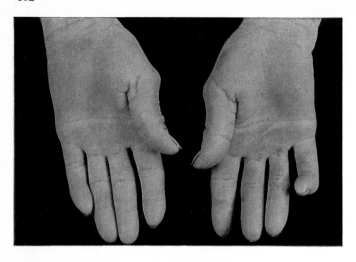

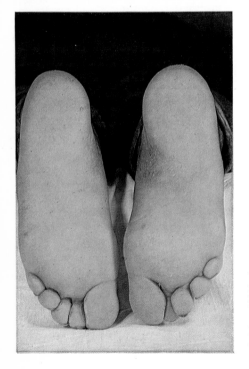

134 and 135 **Keratoma palmare et plantare hereditarium (Unna-Thost).** Keratosis palmaris et plantaris with hard horny masses of even thickness.

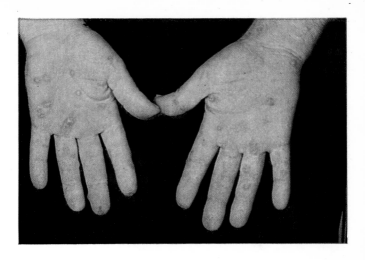

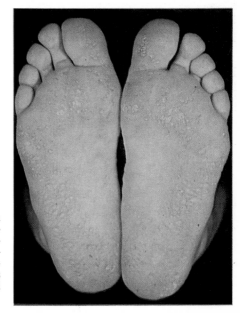

136 and **137 Keratoma palmare et plantare dissipatum hereditarium.** Discrete and coalescent, cone-shaped, hyperkeratotic lesions with erythematous border on the soles and palms.

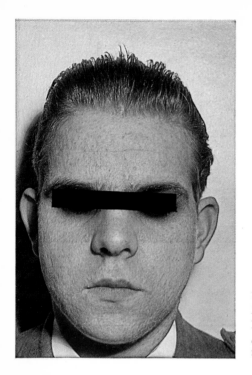

138 **Keratosis follicularis (Darier)**. Coalescing yellowish-brown papules with irregular greasy crusts covering the entire face.

Epidermolysis Bullosa Dystrophica

Inherited as a recessive or dominant trait, this disorder is characterized by bulla formation following even the slightest degree of traumatization. Other important features are scarring, keloids, milia, dystrophic nails or anonychia, erosions and leukokeratosis of the mucous membranes, hyperkeratosis of palms and soles (hyperplastic type of Touraine), skeletal anomalies, impairment of dentition (polydysplastic type of Touraine), and psychological alteration.

Familial Benign Chronic Pemphigus (Hailey-Hailey)

This disease is transmitted by a single dominant gene. In young adults, rapidly eroding vesicles appear on the nape and lateral aspects of the neck, the axillae (Fig. 149), and the genital area. Coalescence of the lesions results in eczematoid, macerated, crusted lesions, which show a tendency to heal spontaneously from the center. Remissions and recurrences alternate.

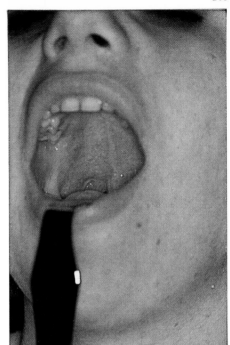

139 Keratosis follicularis (Darier). Small flat papules of the palate. Mucosal lesions are not uncommon.

140 Keratosis follicularis (Darier). Typical involvement of the upper back at the interscapular region. Large hyperkeratotic area with peripheral discrete and coalescent greasy grayish-brown papules.

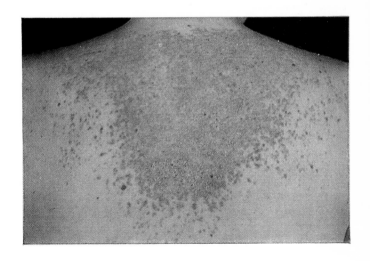

141 Adenoma sebaceum (Pringle). Small, reddish-yellow, firm nodules surrounded by normal skin on the nose and cheek.

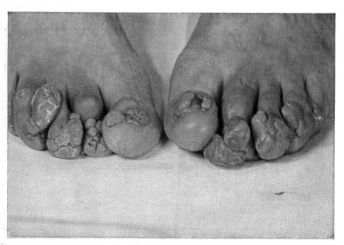

142 Adenoma sebaceum (Pringle). Typical large fibromas (Koenen's periungual tumors).

3 Neurofibromatosis (von Reck-ghausen). Numerous soft neuro-romas which may be depressed ︀o the skin in "push-button" ︀hion. Also, typical "café au lait" ︀ts.

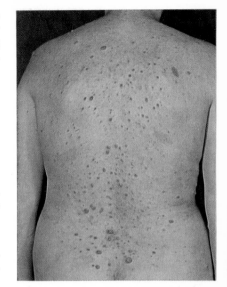

4 Neurofibromatosis (von Reck-ghausen). With large pendulous ︀n flaps (dermatolysis).

5 Pseudoxanthoma elasticum. ︀oups of slightly raised, soft yel-︀wish papules on the lateral aspects ︀the neck.

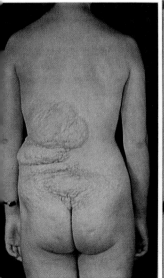

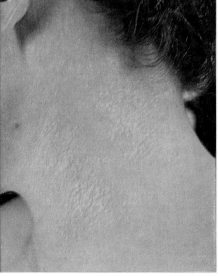

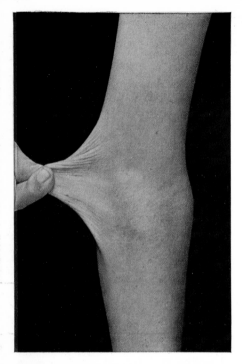

146 Cutis hyperelastica (Ehlers-Danlos).

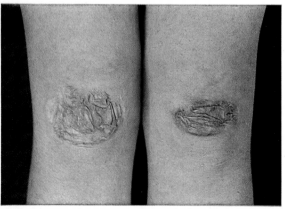

147 Cutis hyperelastica (Ehlers-Danlos). Increased fragility of the skin resulting in atrophic scars.

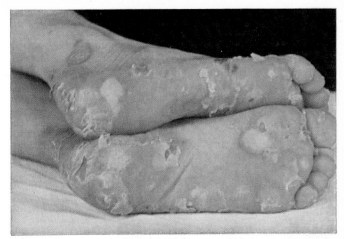

148 Epidermolysis bullosa simplex. Ruptured large bullae and lamelliform scaling of the soles.

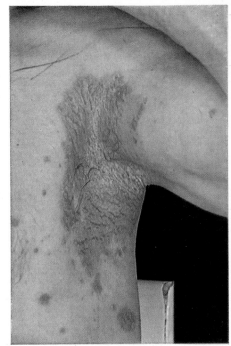

149 Familial benign chronic pemphigus (Hailey-Hailey). Eczematoid, macerated lesions with small peripheral vesicles.

Vesiculobullous Eruptions

Bullae associated with cutaneous diseases of known etiology (bullous syphilid, bullous reactions associated with erysipelas, impetigo, burns, frostbite, insect bites, and allergic reactions of the skin), as well as heritable bullous dermatoses and bullous variants of dermatoses usually characterized by a different morphological pattern, have been described in their respective chapters. This section is devoted to bullous dermatoses of unknown etiology.

Dermatoses with Acantholytic Blister Formation (Pemphigus Group)

Acantholysis resulting in intraepidermal bullae (Civatte, Darier, Tzanck, Lever) is the histological criterion of this group. Detached acantholytic cells can be found within the bullae. These cells are rounded and smaller than normal epidermal cells; their nuclei are large; the cytoplasm is condensed and basophilic. Direct and indirect immunofluorescent staining techniques are also useful in the classification of bullous disorders. The pemphigus group shows intercellular fluorescent antibodies.

Pemphigus Vulgaris

Large blisters may occur in any body region (Fig. 150). Occasionally the first lesions appear on the oral mucosa (Fig. 151), more rarely on the conjunctivae, without significant systemic impairment. The bullae arise on nonerythematous, clinically normal skin; initially they are tense, later they become flaccid. Firm lateral pressure causes the bullae to spread into the surrounding normal skin (Nikolsky's sign). Their clear contents may be hemorrhagic at times. Secondary infection results in cloudy fluid, and may produce an inflammatory erythema in the surrounding skin. The bullae rupture readily, producing painful, easily bleeding erosions on skin and mucous membranes, sometimes associated with crust formation. Without massive doses of corticosteroids, this autoimmune disease progressively leads to secondary systemic involvement, cachexia, and death.

Pemphigus Foliaceus

In this rare disorder, insignificant flaccid vesicles are followed by moist scaling and flaking of the skin surface without visible bullae (Abb. 152). The lesions spread slowly and may involve the entire body surface, resembling a generalized exfoliative dermatitis. This i rarely seen in other types of pemphigus.

Occasionally, pemphigus foliaceus may evolve from pemphigus vulgaris. Nikolsky's sign is positive; the mucous membranes are often involved. Malodorous secondary infection of the skin and loss of hair and nails are commonly seen. Impairment of general health is found only in more advanced stages of the disease.

Brazilian Pemphigus
(Fogo Selvagem)

This condition closely resembles pemphigus foliaceus. It occurs as a febrile, endemic, possibly contagious disease in tropical regions of South America.

Pemphigus Erythematosus (Senear-Usher)

The erythematous, scaling and crusted lesions are clinically suggestive of seborrheic dermatitis (pemphigus seborrhoicus) or lupus erythematosus. They occur mostly in the "butterfly" area of the face. Small bullae also can be seen on the chest and extremities. Nikolsky's sign is positive. The disease takes a relatively benign course, and may even heal completely. In other cases, recurrent progressive exacerbations eventually lead to the clinical picture of pemphigus foliaceus.

Pemphigus Vegetans (Neumann)

This rare and often fatal febrile variety of pemphigus shows a preference for the oral or vulvar mucous membranes and for the intertriginous areas of the axillae, groin (Fig. 153), anogenital, and inframammary regions, where it usually forms fetid, purulent, hypertrophic vegetative masses. Erosions develop less frequently than in other types of pemphigus.

Dermatoses with Subepidermal Blister Formation

Subepidermal bullae without acantholytic cells can be seen in many skin diseases (e.g., erythema multiforme, porphyria, epidermolysis bullosa). The histological findings are not diagnostic.

Bullous Pemphigoid

In this relatively benign and often self-limited disease of elderly people, large and tense, slightly pruritic, nongrpoued bullae appear on erythematous, often edematous skin, chiefly on the lateral aspects of the neck, in the axillae, and on the inner aspects of the thighs. Mucous membrane lesions are rare. The disorder can be differentiated from dermatitis herpetiformis by its onset late in life, absence of grouped lesions, and poor response to sulfapyridine therapy. Differentiation from pemphigus vulgaris is made histologically (subepidermal bullae). Chronic course and absence of target lesions exclude erythema multiforme. Drug eruptions must be ruled out. Bullous pemphigoid has a more favorable prognosis than pemphigus vulgaris; the general health is usually not impaired, except in the aged. Involvement of the subepithelial basement zone can be demonstrated with fluorescent antibody techniques.

Dermatitis Herpetiformis (Duhring)

Recurrent polymorphous eruptions, accompanied by intense itching or burning and eosinophilia of the peripheral blood and blister fluid, are characteristic of dermatitis herpetiformis. Herpetiform grouping, symmetrical arrangement, and characteristic appearance of the lesions are distinctive features. Grouped vesicles arise on an erythematous or urticarial base, usually on the extremities and the trunk, in a symmetrical pattern (Figs. 154—156). In other cases, the lesions may be small, indurated papules or crusted vesicles. Gyrate, erythematous sometimes urticarial patches are often seen initially. The mucous membranes may be involved. Hyperpigmented areas are late sequelae indicative of preceding active lesions.

The disease is more common in male than in female patients, and may occur at any age: usually it appears in middle adult life. Repeated outbreaks are the rule, but spontaneous remissions can be expected in many patients. In elderly persons, Duhring's disease may be a manifestation of internal cancer.

Bullous and Pustular Dermatoses Associated with Pregnancy

Herpes Gestationis (Milton)

This is a rare papular or vesicular eruption of unknown etiology (Fig. 157). It is probably a variant of dermatitis herpetiformis affecting women during pregnancy. In some instances, Rh incompatibility has been demonstrated. The disease usually manifests itself during the first three months of gestation, and disappears soon after delivery. Rarely, it may appear postpartum and persist for several weeks.

Impetigo Herpetiformis (Hebra, Kaposi)

This exceedingly rare disease predominantly affects pregnant women, usually during the last trimester, but may also occur following thyroid operations, or even in male patients. In most cases, grouped pustules

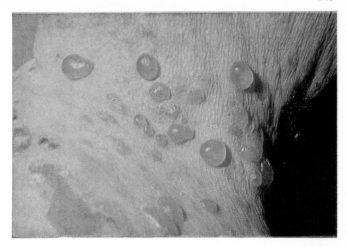

150 Pemphigus vulgaris. Large tense bullae, containing clear fluid and surrounded by clinically normal skin.

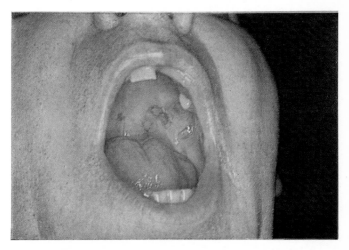

151 Pemphigus vulgaris. Bullae, mostly eroded, on the oral mucosa.

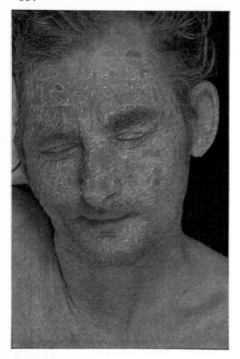

152 Pemphigus foliaceus. Flaking, scaly, erythematous skin without visible bullae or vesicles.

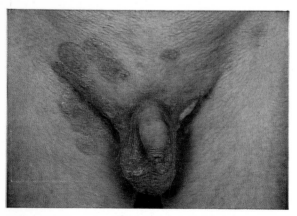

153 Pemphigus vegetans. Well circumscribed, moist hypertrophic patches of the inguinal and genital regions. No macroscopic vesiculation.

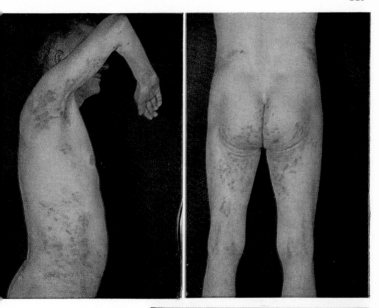

154 and 155 Dermatitis herpetiformis (Duhring). Recurrent, symmetrical polymorphous eruption with herpetiform grouping of individual lesions in typical anatomical distribution.

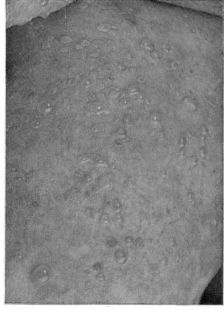

156 Dermatitis herpetiformis (Duhring). Close-up of individual vesicular, urticarial, and erythematous lesions.

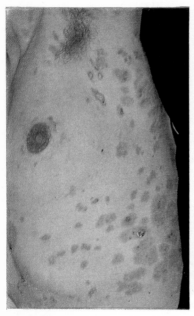

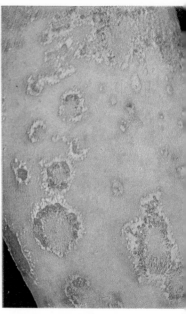

157 Herpes gestationis. Large, erythematous and bullous lesions in a pregnant woman.

158 Impetigo herpetiformis. Close-u view of erythematous grouped pustule in annular arrangement. New pustule arising predominantly in periphery o old lesions.

on an erythematous base, often arranged in rings (Fig. 158), particularly involve intertriginous areas. Differentiation from psoriasi pustulosa is extremely difficult; possibly, impetigo herpetiformi during pregnancy is merely a pustular form of psoriasis. Some case seem to be identical with dermatitis herpetiformis. Other finding suggest an endocrinological pathogenesis of the disease, particularl the presence of severe systemic symptoms and the fatal outcome o some cases. Maceration, secondary infection, nephritis, and diarrhe are associated symptoms. Serum calcium levels are often decreased

Vascular Reaction Patterns

Urticaria

Wheals (urticae) may be produced by toxic or allergic mechanisms. Contact with certain plants or insect bites results in localized urticarial reactions confined to the site of contact with the irritant. Urticaria distributed symmetrically over the entire integument usually is of endogenous origin (ingestants, drugs). The lesions, initially pink, turn white for a short time due to increasing osmotic pressure (compression of capillaries) in the edematous tisue, and finally become pale red wheals again. They often disappear in minutes to hours, and are followed by new lesions. Central healing or coalescence of the eruptions may produce annular or gyrate forms (Fig. 159). Bullous or hemorrhagic wheals are seen occasionally. *Acute urticaria* is usually due to antigen-antibody reactions induced by food or drug allergens. After elimination of the causative agent, the wheals usually subside within a few days. *Chronic urticaria* is characterized by recurrent outbreaks over longer periods of time, usually without demonstrable relationship to ingestion of food or drugs (Fig. 160). Intestinal parasites, functional disturbances in the intestinal tract, allergens, and histamine liberators may be of etiological significance. Physical irritants, such as mechanical injury (Fig. 161), cold, heat, and actinic effects also must be considered.

Quincke's Edema
(Angioneurotic Edema)

Circumscribed subcutaneous edema with a sudden onset usually appears asymmetrically on normal or slightly erythematous skin. The lesions are tense, but not pruritic, and have a predilection for the eyelids, lips, mucous membranes (Fig. 162), and genitals. Drugs or foods must be considered as causative factors. In the presence of edema of the larynx, there is danger of suffocation.

118

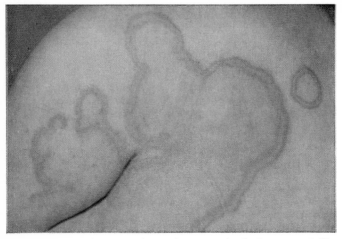

159 Acute urticaria. Annular and gyrate wheals due to penicillin hypersensitivity.

160 Chronic urticaria of unknown origin. Urticarial plaques with active borders and healing centers.

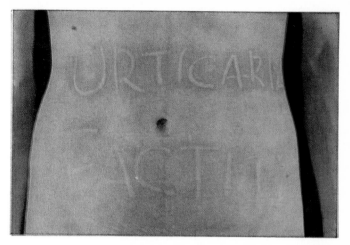

161 Factitial urticaria. Due to pressure. Raised white urticarial areas surrounded by erythematous flare.

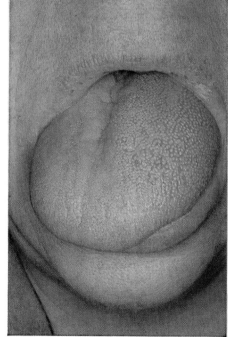

162 Quincke's edema. Massive swelling of the left portion of the tongue.

Diseases of the Cutaneous Blood Vessels

Livedo Reticularis and Livedo Racemosa

These are disorders of deep subcutaneous vessels.

Livedo reticularis is characterized clinically by a permanent blotchy, reticulated, livid red discoloration; etiologically, it is based on disturbances of hormonal and autonomic regulatory mechanisms. It is usually seen on the lower extremities (Fig. 163), less often on the buttocks. The vascular changes are accentuated in cold environment. *Livedo racemosa* shows an arborized pattern of bluish red discoloration (Fig. 164). The skin alteration is due to inflammatory changes of the small arteries and veins of the subcutaneous plexus which may lead to complete occlusion. Arteriosclerosis, hypertension, periarteritis nodosa, thrombangiitis obliterans, syphilis, and tuberculosis may play a pathogenetic role in the development of livedo racemosa. Cryoglobulins may be present.

Thromboangiitis Obliterans (Winiwarter-Buerger)
(Endangiitis Obliterans)

The most important symptoms af this rare inflammatory disorder of the blood vessels are intermittent claudication, diminished pulsations, discoloration, and coldness of the involved extremity. The disease starts with thickening of the intima and obliteration of the lumen by thrombi. Frequently, arterial changes are preceded by involvement of the veins in the form of *phlebitis saltans* (Fig. 165). The etiology of thromboangiitis obliterans is unknown. It has its highest incidence in men between 20 and 40 years of age, particularly in heavy smokers. Veins and arteries of the lower legs, feet (Fig. 166) and fingers are most often affected, usually in unilateral distribution.

Allergic Cutaneous Vasculitis (Ruiter)

Hemorrhagic or bluish red subcutaneous nodules and papulonecrotic lesions are seen in this disorder (Fig. 167). Focal infections and drug allergies have been discussed as etiologic factors. Other forms of allergic vasculitis are *nodular dermal allergid* (Gougerot), and *erythema elevatum diutinum;* probably also *pityriasis lichenoides et varioliformis acuta* (Mucha-Habermann) and *dermatitis nodularis necrotica* (Werther-Duemling).

Arteriosclerosis Obliterans

(Endangiosis Arteriosclerotica)

Calcification and necrosis of the medial coat and sclerotic changes of the intima of the arteries, usually seen in men over 50 years of age, produce changes on the extremities that are difficult to differentiate clinically from thromboangiitis obliterans. In the presence of arteriosclerotic changes, diabetes mellitus should be ruled out. The most common symptoms are intermittent claudication, postural color changes, coolness, diminished pulsations, atrophy, and hair loss of the distal parts of the extremities (Fig. 168).

Diabetic Gangrene

Diabetic angiolopathy is the cause of diabetic gangrene. In most cases, only 1 or 2 toes are involved; or the gangrene may start on the dorsal aspect of the foot or on the heel. The primary lesion is a small painful nodule. Edema, exudation, and central necrosis, accompanied by a pronounced tendency to secondary infection, rapidly lead to the development of gangrenous changes (Fig. 169). Vascular occlusion often is confined to superficial vessels.

Varicose Veins and Chronic Venous Insufficiency

Dilatations of veins in the lower extremities, especially of the medial surfaces, may be associated with or followed by *stasis dermatitis*, *thrombophlebitis*, sclerosis of connective tissue, pachyderma, sclerotic atrophy (*atrophie blanche* [Milian]), scarring, hyperpigmentation, petechiae, and hemosiderin deposits. The most disturbing sequelae of varicose veins are *stasis ulcers* (Fig. 170).

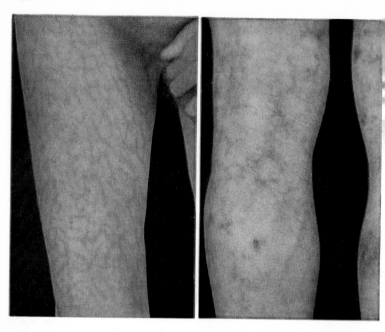

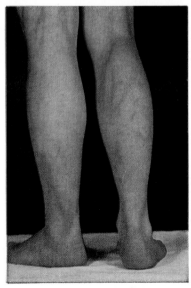

163 Livedo reticularis. Blotchy, reticulated, livid-red discoloration, accentuated by cold environment.

164 Livedo racemosa. Associated with periarteritis nodosa.

165 Phlebitis saltans. Band-like erythema and infiltration over veins.

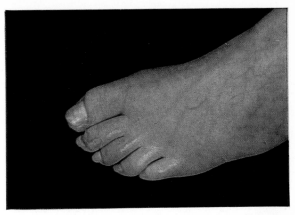

166 Thromboangiitis obliterans. Necroses in cold, atrophic, shiny skin.

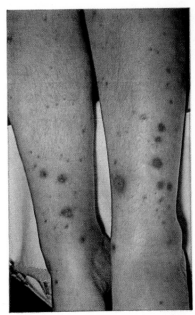

167 Allergic cutaneous vasculitis. Discrete red patches with necrotic centers.

124

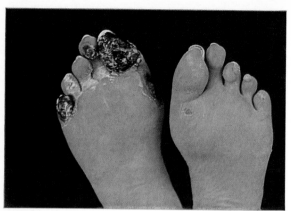

168 Arteriosclerosis obliterans. Severe necroses of the toes, associated with diminished pulsations, coolness, and atrophy of the skin, and intermittent claudication.

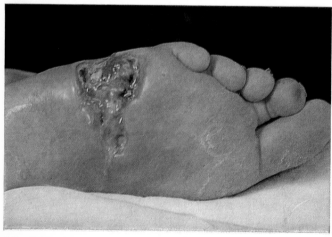

169 Diabetic gangrene. Painful, large ulcer with secondary infection.

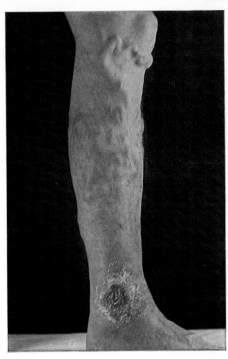

170 Varicose veins and stasis ulcer. Large tortuous varicose veins with recurrent stasis ulcer of medial malleolar area.

Diseases of the Skin Appendages

Diseases of the Sebaceous Glands

Acne Vulgaris

Acne usually manifests itself before and during puberty, and may persist well into the third decade. The disorder affects face, chest, back, and neck, i.e., skin areas amply supplied with sebaceous glands. Increased sebum production and keratinous obstruction of the follicular orifices with comedones result in the typical clinical picture of acne which is usually polymorphous; clear-cut forms of *comedo acne*, *papular acne* (Fig. 171), *pustular acne*, and *acne indurata* (Fig. 172) are rare. Severe forms extending deep into the cutis may heal with characteristic "ice pick" scars.

The relationship between acne vulgaris and endocrine factors is well established. Testosterone, ACTH, and cortisone and its derivates stimulate sebum secretion, and are capable of producing acne lesions in certain patients. Other etiological factors are still unknown.

In contrast to acne vulgaris, *acne conglobata* is not confined to any particular age group. It occurs predominantly in men, involving back, gluteal area, and neck, less often the face. The nuchal lesions are identical with folliculitis et perifolliculitis capitis abscedens et suffodiens. The clinical picture of acne conglobata is characterized by indolent deep-seated abscesses, ulcerations, giant or double comedones, and various types of scarring (Fig. 173).

Acneform Eruption Due to Drugs or Occupational Factors

As has been mentioned above, certain steroids are capable of inducing acne. Bromides and iodides may aggravate preexisting acne vulgaris or induce "bromine acne" or "iodine acne", which is not preceded by comedones.

Nodular and vegetative eruptions in other areas are known as *bromoderma* (Fig. 174) or *ioderma tuberosum*.

Exogenous and endogenous action of chlorinated industrial products may cause severe skin changes, such as comedones, pustules, and sebum retention cysts on face, neck (Fig. 175), chest, back, and extremities (halogen acne); these agents also may induce parenchymatous liver damage. Another form of occupational acne is *"oil acne"* caused by contact with mineral oils.

A peculiar form of acne is *"acne excoriée des jeunes filles"* (Brocq). The patients have a neurotic habit of picking their faces and expressing minimal acne lesions. As a result, the face is covered with numerous excoriations and flat pigmented scars (Fig. 176). Local treatment must be supported by psychological guidance directed at normalizing the patient's behavior.

Rosacea and Rhinophyma

Rosacea is a chronic hyperemic disorder based on a seborrheic condition. It occurs chiefly in middle-aged patients. The disorder starts with vasodilatation in the flush area of the face; the involved area later assumes a blotchy dusky red to purple discoloration. In addition, there are patulous follicular orifices and telangiectases on cheeks and nose, often associated with edema, greasy papules, and minute pustules (Fig. 177). These lesions prompted the name "acne rosacea", although they are not directly related to acne vulgaris; comedones are absent. In the presence of inflammatory granulomata and marked development of papules, the disorder is called hypertrophic rosacea. Conjunctivitis and keratitis may be concomitant features. Tumorous deformation of the nose associated with marked proliferation of sebaceous glands results in the thickened, lobulated *rhinophyma* (Fig. 178), which is more common in men than in women.

Rosacea develops on the basis of constitutional irregularities manifested by seborrhea and disturbances of vasomotor function. It may be triggered or supported by menopause, internal diseases, achlorhydria, gastric ulcers, intestinal or hepatic disorders, emotional abnormalities, ingestants (alcohol, coffee, tea, hot spices), external irritants, and local action of heat.

Differential diagnosis includes seborrheic dermatitis, acute and subacute lupus erythematosus, sarcoidosis, syphilis and tuberculosis miliaris disseminata faciei.

Diseases of the Hair: Alopecia

Congenital alopecia is usually irreversible. Easily confused with *alopecia congenita circumscripta* is *aplasia congenita circumscripta*; in this disorder, the skin is not developed in circumscribed areas, which have the appearance of ulcerations or scars.

Alopecia areata (Sauvage) usually has a sudden onset, occasionally preceded by headaches and neuralgia. There is complete loss of hair in sharply defined round or oval patches, usually without any visible erythema or other skin changes (Fig. 173). In milder cases, new hair growth may occur spontaneously after 4 or 5 months (Fig. 180). Alopecia areata usually remains confined to isolated patches of the scalp, but it may also involve the entire scalp (alopecia totalis), the beard, eyebrows, and eyelashes. In rare cases, a universal alopecia may develop. Typically, dystrophic hairs, 2 to 3 mm. long and with flattened dark tips (exclamation point hairs), surround the bald spots in alopecia areata. Dystrophic nail changes may also occur.

Telogen effluvium (Kligman) is a reversible form of hair loss. All the hairs shed (often suddenly and in great numbers) are club hairs (telogen hairs). The most common types are neonatal, postfebrile (e.g., scarlet fever), postpartum, and psychogenic effluvium. Some drugs, especially heparinoids (Fig. 184), may also induce telogen effluvium. Hair loss usually starts 6 to 12 weeks following the onset of the stress situation. Regrowth may not occur for several months. (Normal hair of the scalp grows 3 mm. in 10 days.)

Dystrophic anagen effluvium is another type of reversible hair loss with predominantly dystrophic anagen hairs. It is seen as a side effect of chemotherapy with cytotoxic drugs, or after systemic poisons (Fig. 181). Hair loss usually starts shortly after the injury; it is often more massive than telogen effluvium and may involve almost all growing hair follicles.

Cicatricial alopecia is an irreversible process due to destruction of the hair papillae by local trauma or by chronic inflammatory or scarring diseases of the scalp (e.g., chronic radiodermatitis [Fig. 182], scleroderma, chronic discoid lupus erythematosus, lupus vulgaris, lichen planus, folliculitis decalvans, and follicular infections).

Pseudopelade (Brocq) is characterized by marked atrophy of the scalp and loss of hair follicles in multiple coin-sized irregular patches with finger-like projections and "onion skin" surface. Some authors believe pseudopelade do be identical with follicular atrophic lichen planus (lichen planopilaris) of the scalp (Graham-Little syndrome).

Disorders of the Nails

Pits, furrows, streaks, or bands of the nail plate may be caused by external or internal factors. The actual time of the injury can be estimated as follows: The normal nails grows 1 mm. in 10 days. Eight weeks pass until the new nail becomes visible; 5 to 6 months until the distal end is reached. It should be considered, however, that the rate of nail growth varies in different periods of life, and that fingernails always grow faster than toenails.

Pitted Nails

Tiny surface pits of the nail plate are characteristic of psoriasis, but also may be associated with dermatitis, alopecia areata, and other disorders involving the nail matrix.

Nail Changes in Psoriasis Arthropathica

Deformities of hands and feet are usually associated with severe dystrophic changes of the nail plate.

Clubbing of the Nails
(Hippocratic Nails)

Clubbed fingers and the associated clubbing, thickening, and increased convexity of the nails are seen primarily in chronic pulmonary and cardiac disorders.

Transverse Furrows
(Beau's Lines)

Severe systemic stress (febrile infectious diseases, allergic or toxic disorders [Figs. 183 and 184], nutritional deficiencies, severe shock, and local trauma or skin diseases) may cause temporary impairment of nail growth manifested in shallow or deep transverse furrows or grooves.

Mees' Lines

Mees' lines are a variety of leukonychia striata in which a single white transverse band can be observed in all the nails. It used to be seen following arsenic or thallium poisoning, but it may also occur in febrile illnesses, Hodgkin's disease, severe cardiac disorders and many other systemic diseases.

Longitudinal Ridges

Accentuation of the normal longitudinal ridges of the nail plate is primarily a senile manifestation. Longitudinal fractures or splitting of the nail plate occur less frequently and are independent of age. Chronic radiodermatitis may induce similar nail changes. Occupational factors are also important.

Onycholysis

Gradual separation of the nail plate from the nail bed starting at the distal edge results in a half-moon or pocket shaped free space beneath the whitish nail plate. This may be due to various external factors, such as moist work, alkalis, and faulty manicuring techniques.

Subungual Hyperkeratoses

Subungual hyperkeratoses with separation of the nail plate may be associated with chronic dermatitis, psoriasis, pityriasis rubra pilaris, and onychomycosis.

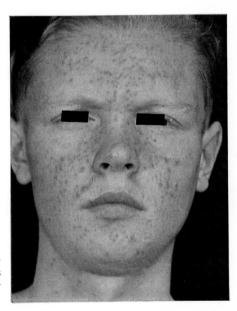

171 Acne vulgaris. Many papules, with some pustules and comedones in characteristic localization.

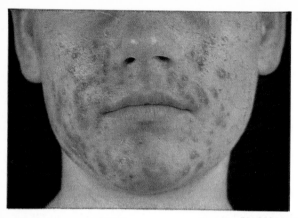

172 Acne vulga
(acne indurata).
Deeply indurated,
nodular, papular,
and pustular lesio
with characteristic
small "ice pick"
scars.

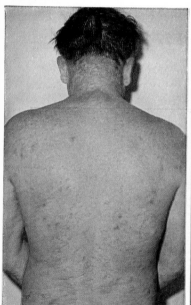

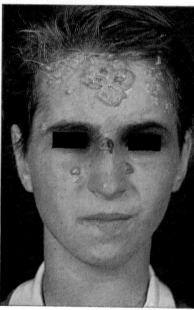

173 Acne conglobata. Deep-seated
indolent cysts resulting in severe
scarring. Often associated with large
comedones.

174 Bromoderma tuberosum. Circumscribed nodular and vegetative
crusted lesions of the face.

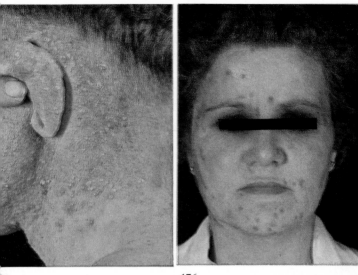

175   176

175 Occupational acne. Severe eruption with numerous comedones, papules, pustules and crusts due to exposure to tetrachlordibenzodioxin ("halogen acne").

176 Acne excoriée des jeunes filles. Multiple excoriations and scars due to neurotic habit of picking minimal acne lesions.

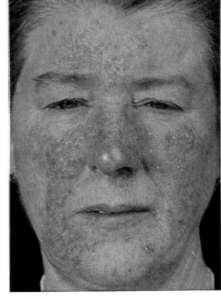

177 Rosacea. Erythema, papular infiltration, slight desquamation, blepharitis, and conjunctivitis. No comedones.

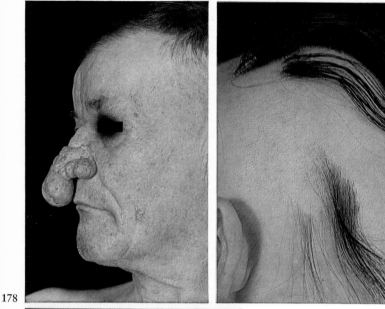

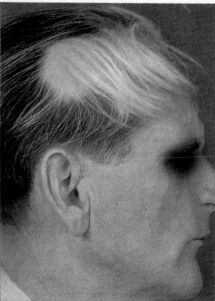

178 Rhinophyma.
Grotesque, lobulated, proliferative growth of the nose in a patient with rosacea.

179 Alopecia areata. No atrophy; the follicular orifices are clearly visible. Some short "exclamation point" hairs in center of the picture.

180 Alopecia areata. Regrowth of nonpigmented hairs.

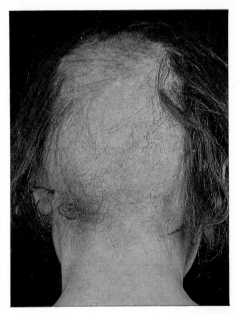

181 Anagen effluvium.
Almost complete hair loss following ingestion of rat poison containing thallium. Most hairs show dystrophic anagen hair roots. In contrast to telogen effluvium, hair loss starts shortly after injury.

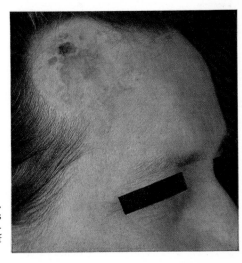

182 Cicatricial alopecia.
Chronic radiodermatitis with radiation ulcer following X-ray treatment of lupus vulgaris.

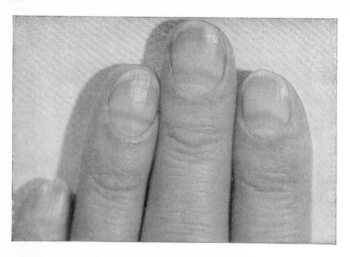

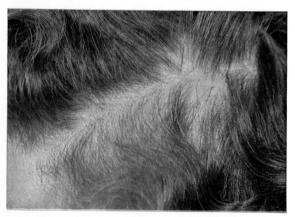

183 and **184** **Transverse furrows (Beau's lines).** The nail changes followed heparin treatment and were accompanied by massive diffuse loss of telogen hairs (telogen effluvium).

Onychogryphosis

Claw-like deformation of the nails, usually limited to the large toe nails, is not infrequently seen in older patients. The nails are hard and markedly thickened, twisted and curved. Simultaneously, there is marked subungual hyperkeratosis. Local pressure, deformities of the foot, and local circulatory disturbances may be responsible for this abnormality. Claw nails on the fingers are rare.

Diseases of the Corium

Striae Atrophicae

Slightly depressed, bluish-red (later white), shiny smooth atrophic lines in a parallel or fan-shaped arrangement may occur in the abdominal region, on the buttocks, the thighs, and the breasts in association with pregnancy or rapid growth, during or following weight reduction in obesity, in some systemic infections, after long-term corticosteroid treatment, and in Cushing's syndrome. In all these instances, the striae are attributed to increased cortisone production of the adrenal cortex; stretching is believed to play only a secondary role.

Acrodermatitis Chronica Atrophicans (Pick-Herxheimer)

This diesase is seen predominantly on the dorsa of hands and feet, as well as on the forearms and lower legs of women over 40 years of age. An initial inflammatory-edematous stage (Fig. 185) is followed by an atrophic stage (Fig. 186). The skin is easily movable and resembles crumpled cigarette paper; it becomes transparent due to loss of subcutaneous fatty tissue. Deeper blood vessels and tendons become visible, and telangiectases contribute to the characteristic clinical picture of the disease. Late changes include deep fibroid nodules (juxta-articular nodules) and sclerotic areas, often in the form of linear fibrotic bands, predominantly on the lower legs and in the ulnar region (Fig. 187). The cause of Herxheimer's disease is unknown.

Lichen Sclerosus et Atrophicus

Thin, wrinkled, ivory-white, atrophic and sclerotic macules and grouped, polygonal, flat-topped white papules with central delling and follicular plugging may be disseminated over the entire body surface, but usually are confined to the upper trunk and neck or the genital area. In female patients, this leads to the clinical picture of *kraurosis vulvae* (Fig. 188), a chronic sclerotic pruritic process of the vulva, with parchment-like whitish skin changes. In men a similar condition is called *kraurosis penis* or *balanitis xerotica obliterans* (Fig. 189).

Localized Scleroderma
(Morphea)

Morphea is most common on the trunk of young patients and takes a benign course. The disease starts with a round or oval, circumscribed, slightly erythematous, smooth plaque with a firm white sclerotic center. The lesion spreads peripherally and is surrounded by a typical violaceous halo (Fig. 190). The skin appendages in the involved areas become atrophic.

Linear forms are seen on forehead and scalp (en coup de sabre) (Fig. 191) and on the extremities; they may be associated with atrophy of muscle and bone.

Diffuse Systemic Sclerosis
(Progressive Systemic Scleroderma)

Progressive or diffuse systemic scleroderma has a grave prognosis. Involving the connective tissue and the blood vessels, the disease manifests itself not only on the skin, but also in internal organs (esophagus, lungs, heart, kidney, skeletal system).

From the dermatological aspect, the clinical picture is dominated by typical sclerodermic changes, associated with hyperpigmentation, atrophic ulcers, and telangiectases, particularly on the hands (claw-like fingers) (Fig. 192) feet, and neck. The face is expressionless due to restricted mobility.

Dermatomyositis (Wagner-Unverricht)

This grave disease is more common in middle-aged females; it involves skin and muscles, especially of the face, neck, arms, and legs (Fig. 193). Nonspecific diffuse or macular, often edematous, mostly symmetrically arranged erythematous lesions usually appear first on the face (Fig. 194) — frequently with characteristic "heliotrope bloating" of the upper eyelids. Weakness, tenderness, and atrophy of shoulder and hip muscles are suggestive symptoms. In most cases there is involvement of internal organs (heart, lungs, intestinal tract, kidneys). Internal neoplasms (usually adenocarcinomas) should be ruled out in all adult patients with dermatomyositis.

The poikilodermatic type runs a more chronic course. Pigmentary changes, diffuse atrophy, and teleangiectasia are its characteristics (Fig. 195).

Chronic Discoid Lupus Erythematosus

In chronic discoid lupus erythematosus, sharply outlined inflammatory, nonpruritic, erythematous, scaling plaques with follicular hyperkeratoses spread peripherally, leaving central atrophy, telangiectasia and scarring (Figs. 196 and 197). The disease is aggravated by sunlight, and is usually seen in exposed areas of the face (often in characteristic "butterfly" distribution), ears, neck, scalp, and arms. Its incidence is highest in middle-aged persons, somewhat higher in women than in men. In rare cases, multiple typical discoid patches may occur on the trunk and other body areas in the form of a widespread, disseminate, chronic discoid lupus erythematosus (Fig. 198). The etiology of the disease is unknown; systemic symptoms are usually absent.

Acute Systemic Lupus Erythematosus
(Kaposi-Libman-Sacks-Syndrome)

Very rarely, acute systemic lupus erythematosus may evolve from chronic discoid lupus erythematosus; usually, it occurs without preceding skin changes. The disease has a higher incidence in young females. It starts with erythematous patches on the face (Fig. 199) and the hands (fingertips), accompanied by fever and malaise. The symptomatology of acute systemic lupus erythematosus also includes endocarditis, polyserositis, myalgia, arthritis, glomerulonephritis, central nervous system disorders (convulsions), and mucous membrane involvement. Hematologic findings include leukopenia, lupus erythematosus (L. E.) cells (Hargraves), the L.E. factor (Haserick), elevation of serum gamma globulins, and antinuclear antibodies. In general, the prognosis is unfavorable, although subacute and chronic cases extending over 10 to 20 years have been reported. Autoimmunization reactions are believed to play a role in the pathogenesis of the disease.

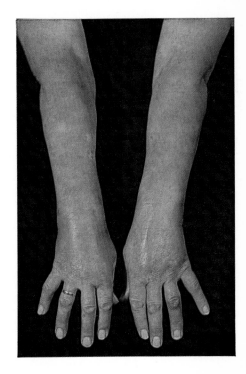

185 Acrodermatitis chronica atrophicans (Pick-Herxheimer). Early, inflammatory, edematous stage with beginning "cigarette paper" atrophy of the dorsa of the hands.

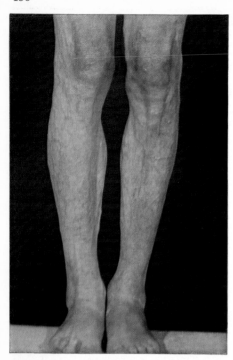

186 Acrodermatitis chronica atrophicans (Pick-Herxheimer). Advanced atrophic stage. Veins are clearly visible through transparent skin.

187 Acrodermatitis chronica atrophicans (Pick-Herxheimer). Band-like, inflammatory infiltration (ulnar band).

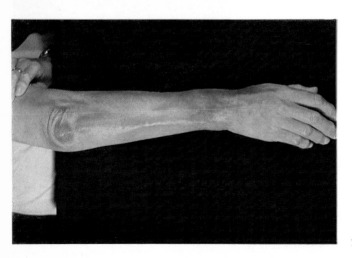

187

139

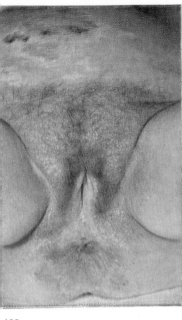
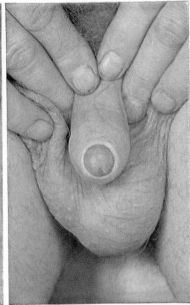

188 189

188 Lichen sclerosus et atrophicus. Extensive involvement of abdomen, vulva, and anal region.

189 Lichen sclerosus et atrophicus. Atrophy of prepuce and glans penis (kraurosis penis; balanitis xerotica obliterans).

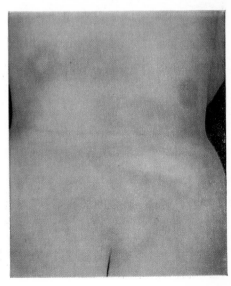

190 Localized scleroderma. Older plaques show peripheral hyperpigmentation; active lesions are characterized by violaceous border.

140

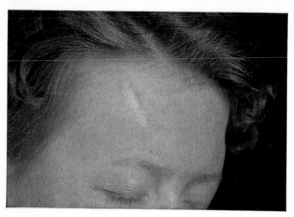

191 Localized scleroderma (en coup de sabre).
Linear lesion on forehead resembling saber scar.

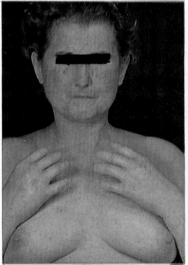

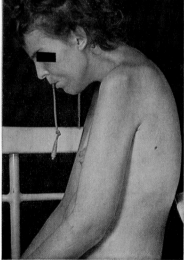

192 Diffuse systemic sclerosis.
Restricted mobility of the face,
numerous telangiectases, clawlike
fingers (sclerodactylia).

193 Dermatomyositis. Characteristic
posture and facial expression of a
patient suffering from severe dermatomyositis.

194 and **195 Dermatomyositis.**
Marked edema of the upper lip,
diffuse erythema of the face, macular erythema of the shoulders, arms,
and upper chest. On the dorsal
aspects of the hands, circumscribed
atrophic patches, telangiectases,
pigmentary changes, and lichenoid
papules (poikilodermic type).

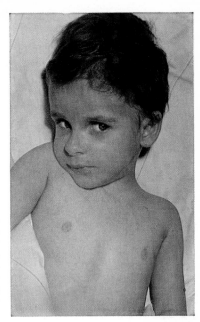

194

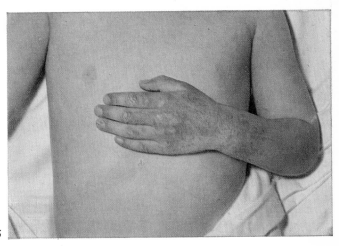

195

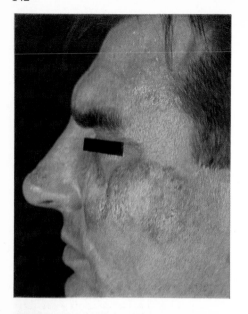

196 Chronic discoid lupus erythematosus.
Sharply outlined, erythematous, scaling plaque with central atrophy, follicular hyperkeratoses, telangiectases, and pigmentary changes in the "butterfly area" of the face.

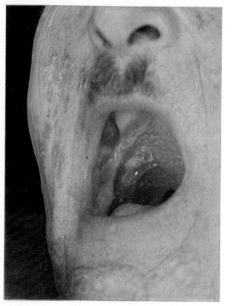

197 Chronic discoid lupus erythemtaosus. Hyperkeratotic lesions of the face and erythematous patches with reticulated, grayish-white discoloration of the oral mucosa.

143

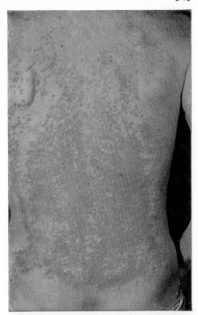

198 Chronic discoid lupus erythematosus. Disseminated form, with discrete and confluent erythematous scaling patches.

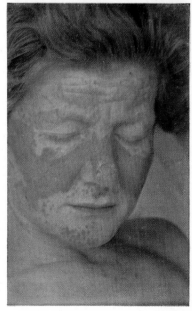

199 Acute systemic lupus erythematosus. Erythematous patches of the butterfly area of the face accompanied by fever and systemic symptoms.

Metabolic Skin Diseases

Xanthomatoses

Xanthomatoses are cutaneous manifestations of anomalies of lipid metabolism. According to their morphologic appearance, they can be classified as follows: *Xanthoma tuberosum* occurs mostly over the extensor surfaces of the joints with grouped yellow to orange colored nodules (Fig. 200). It may be associated with type I or II hyperlipoproteinemia, biliary cirrhosis and myxedema. In *Xanthoma disseminatum*, the predominant lesions are discrete or disseminated papules, which are reddish to yellow in color. They are usually found on the neck, axillae, inguinal fold and trunk. These lesions are seen in the rare normolipoproteinemic mucocutaneous xanthomatosis. This chronic, benign disorder is sometimes associated with diabetes insipidus. In *xanthoma tendinosum* small papules and nodules are found in the tendons, especially on the dorsa of hands and feet and at the achilles tendon. *Eruptive xanthoma* consists of small yellowish brown papules with an erythematous halo, which appear in crops over the entire body; they favor the buttocks and flexor surfaces of arms and thighs. *Xanthoma planum* appears as flat macules or plaques of yellow or orange color, sometimes over large areas. They are more common on the inner surface of the thighs, antecubital and popliteal spaces. Xanthelasma of the eyelids is frequently associated.

Classification of cutaneous xanthomatoses in reference to their gross morphologic appearance is less useful than classification according to changes in blood lipid levels (Frederickson). *Type I hyperlipoproteinemia* is the very rare essential familial hyperlipemia (Bürger-Grütz syndrome) which is characterized by eruptive xanthomas, less often by tuberous xanthomas. It begins in childhood, and is frequently associated with abdominal symptoms. *Type II hyperlipoproteinemia* is also known as essential familial hypercholesterolemia. This dominant disorder is characterized by an elevated serum cholesterol in association with xanthelasma, xanthoma tendinosum and tuberosum, arcus senilis, atherosclerosis and myocardial infarction. Major secondary causes are hypothyroidism, nephrosis and biliary obstruction. In *type III hyperlipoproteinemia*, both cholesterol and triglycerides are markedly increased ("broad beta disease"). The familial type shows distinctive xanthoma planum of the palms, trunk and neck, less often tendon xanthomas and tuberous xanthomas. *Type IV hyperlipoproteinemia* is a common, frequently familial disorder, which is also known as endogenous hypertriglyceridemia. It is often associated with eruptive xanthomas. Major secondary causes include diabetes mellitus, nephrotic syndrome and estrogen imbalance. *Type V hyperlipoproteinemia* presents a rare combination of type I and Type IV, and is often associated with eruptive xanthomas on back, shoulders, and buttocks.

Obesity and hepatosplenomegaly are common complications; pancreatitis, diabetes mellitus and nephrotic syndrome are secondary causes.

Xanthelasma Palpebrarum

Xanthelasma is the most common type of xanthoma. It appears in adult life, forming soft, yellow flat plaques in the eyelids, predominantly on the medial portion of the upper lids. Serum cholesterol levels are elevated in approximately one-half of patients with xanthelasma.

Necrobiosis Lipoidica Diabeticorum (Urbach)

This disease is not confined exclusively to diabetics, although it may precede the appearance of diabetes mellitus by many years. It may occur at any age, more frequently in women than in men, usually involving the anterior surfaces of the lower legs (Fig. 201).

The characteristic plaque is sharply defined, with an atrophic yellowish center and a bluish-violet peripheral zone; the surface is waxy and slightly telangiectatic. These skin changes evolve from inflammatory vascular processes (lipid deposits in necrobiotic collagen).

Localized Pretibial Myxedema

Occasionally intercellular accumulation of mucin, distributed symmetrically over the extensor surfaces of the lower legs and the dorsa of the feet, occurs in hyperthyroidism. The plaque-like lesions are yellowish to reddish-brown (Fig. 202); the follicular openings are dilated (peau d'orange surface). Marked exophthalmos is usually present simultaneously (Fig. 203). The condition also occurs after thyroidectomy.

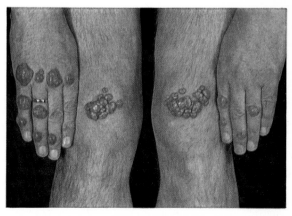

200   Type I hyperlipoproteinemia. Large, yellow, tuberous xanthomas of the knees and hands. These lesions are more common in hypercholesteremic xanthomatosis (type II hyperlipoproteinemia).

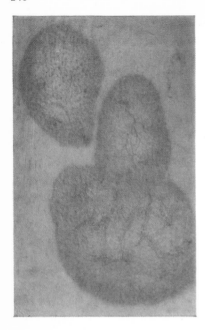

201 Necrobiosis lipoidica diabeticorum. Sharply marginated, yellowish-brown, atrophic plaques on the lower leg with erythematous periphery and central telangiectases.

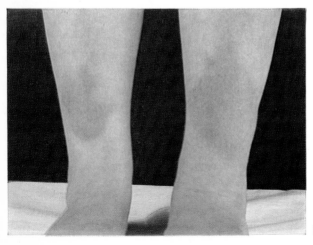

202

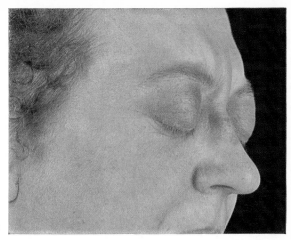

203

202 and **203** **Localized pretibial myxedema.** Symmetrical, infiltrated, reddish-brown plaques on the extensor surface of the lower legs with dilated follicular openings (peau d'orange skin) in hyperthyroid patient with marked exophthalmos.

Gout

Tophi (deposits of sodium urate crystals) usually occur in the form of waxy nodules on the rims of the ears (Fig. 204) and near the distal points of the extremities. They are pathognomonic of chronic gout, a familial disturbance of nucleic acid metabolism, inherited as a dominant trait occuring primarily in men. The nodules may ulcerate and discharge chalky white material.

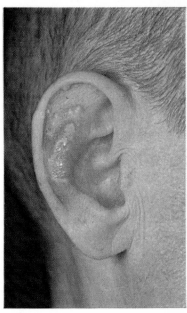

204 Gout. Waxy nodules (tophi) of the ear.

Photodermatoses

All skin changes classified as photodermatoses are induced by exposure to sunlight, and heal when sunlight is eliminated. Ultraviolet rays ranging in wave langths from 280 mμ to 400 mμ and visible rays varying from 400 mμ to 760 mμ, are responsible for these changes. A common dermatosis produced by overexposure to sunlight is *dermatitis solaris* or sunburn. *Phototoxic* substances (oil of bergamot, cumarin — containing essential oils) increase light sensivity and thus lead to pathologic changes, such as *berloque dermatitis* and *dermatitis pratensis* (grass dermatitis) or *phytophotodermatitis*. These reactions can be elicited in most persons.

Photoallergic substances (phenothiazines, sulfonamides, demethylchlortetracycline, clearing agents, p-amino-salicylic acid) induce erythema and bulla formation in light-exposed skin areas of sensitized subjects. An antigen-antibody mechanism is operative in this type of reaction.

Chronic Polymorphous Light Eruptions (Haxthausen)

The clinical picture of chronic polymorphous light eruptions is varied, comprising papular and eczematous as well as temporary erythematous eruptions with edematous infiltration and lupus erythematosus-like patches (Fig. 205). The diagnosis is confirmed by localization of the eruptions in light-exposed areas, remission during fall and winter, and phototests with various light sources after elimination of the erythematogenic range (below 320 mμ) with special filters. Three types of this condition have been described: eczematous, lupus erythematosus-like. and erythematosus light eruption (Wulf).

Actinic Cheilitis
(Summer Cheilitis; Marchionini)

During the hot season, UV-radiation may produce inflammatory erythema, blistering, and crust formation on the lower lip (Fig. 206).

Cutaneous Porphyrias

Congenital Porphyria
(Erythropoietic Porphyria; Günther)

This very rare disease, probably transmitted as a mendelian recessive trait more common in boys than in girls, usually manifests itself soon after birth. Burgundy-red to brown discoloration of the urine may be the first visible sign of the disease. Significant amounts of porphyrin, predominantly uroporphyrin I and coproporphyrin I, but no porphobilinogen are excreted in the urine. Uroporphyrin I, a photosensitizer, is responsible for the rapidly progressive course of the illness which manifests itself clinically as a photodermatosis. In light-exposed areas of the skin, small itching necroses surrounded by erythema appear, develop into vesicles and hemorrhagic blisters (*hydroa aestivale*), and eventually lead to atrophy, ulceration, scarring, hyperpigmentation, and milia; severe mutilations of the ear, nose, eyelids, and fingers (*hydroa vacciniforme*) may result (Fig. 207). Associated symptoms are anemia, splenomegaly, photophobia, conjunctivitis, keratitis, and erythrodontia. Urinary excretion of porphyrin usually is grossly visible, but smaller amounts may be visualized under Wood's light (reddish fluorescence). Some of the red blood cells also fluoresce under Wood's light owing to their high content of uroporphyrin I and coproporphyrin I. The probable cause of this inborn error of metabolism is the lack of a specific enzyme (isomerase).

Porphyria Cutanea Tarda (Waldenström)
(Chronic Hepatic Porphyria (Watson))

Waldenström differentiated between hereditary and symptomatic porphyria cutanea tarda. Some authors attribute the disease to hepatic damage (alcohol) in association with genetic factors. Others assume a disturbance in porphyrin metabolism on the basis of hepatic impairment due to alcohol, arsenic, barbiturates, or hepatitis. The metabolic defect is believed to be due to decarboxylase deficiency of the liver cell. Porphyria cutanea tarda is one of the most common forms of cutaneous porphyria, and is usually seen in males with chronic liver damage in the 40 to 60 age group. Short solar exposure or slight traumatization may produce small vesicles or bullae, which eventually may lead to erosions, crusts, milia, atrophy, flat scars, hypo- or hyperpigmentation, and hypertrichosis (Figs. 208 and 209). Urinary porphyrin levels are increased.

Xeroderma Pigmentosum (Kaposi)

Exposure to sunlight initially produces erythema and scaling, later hyperpigmented spots, and eventually atrophic scars and telangiectases similar to those seen in chronic radiodermatitis. The disease may have its onset in early infancy. Face, neck, upper chest, hands, and forearms are involved. As in chronic radiodermatitis, keratoses and papillomas with a tendency to malignant degeneration (usually carcinomatous) may develop (Fig. 210). The disease is inherited as a recessive gene. Patients in whom it becomes manifest at an early age rarely survive adolescence.

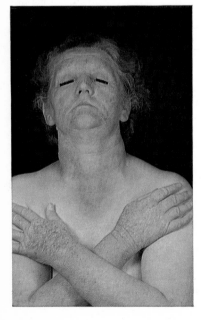

205 Chronic polymorphous light eruption. Lichenification of the face and hands. Typically, the submental area is not affected.

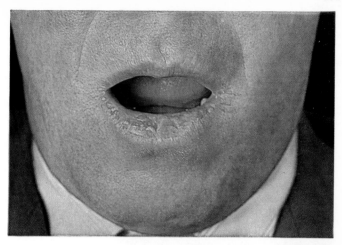

206 **Actinic cheilitis.** Erythema, edema, and scaling of the lower lip.

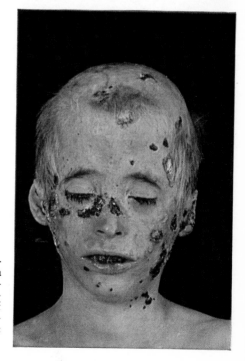

207 **Congenital (erythropoietic) porphyria (hydroa vacciniforme).** Hemorrhagic blisters, crusts, necroses, and scars in areas of face exposed to light associated with systemic symptoms.

152

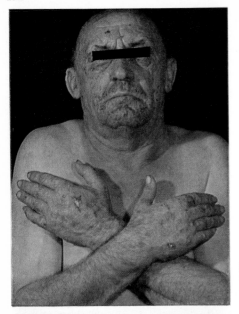

208 **Porphyria cutanea tarda.** Hepatic porphyria with crusted lesions of the face and hands.

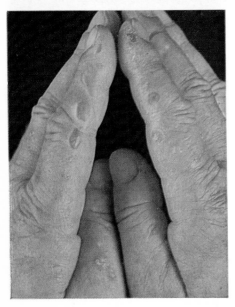

209 **Porphyria cutenea tarda.** Vesicles, crusts, and shallow scars.

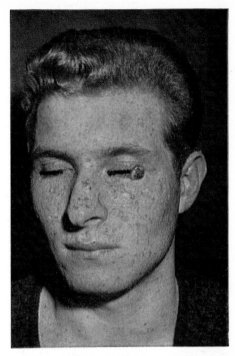

210 Xeroderma pigmentosum. Typical atrophic skin changes resembling chronic radiodermatitis. Squamous cell carcinoma on the left lower eyelid.

Reactions to Physical and Chemical Agents

Mechanical injury including pressure, friction, and rubbing may, unde certain conditions, provoke pigmentation, blistering, and hyper keratoses of the skin. Constant pressure may lead to local anemia and necrosis of the skin (decubitus).

Thermal burns are caused by open flame, hot vapors, molten metals or radiant heat; *scalds* are caused by hot liquids. First-degree burns o scalds are characterized by erythema; second-degree injuries by bliste formation; and third-degree injuries by necrosis. Determination of the depth and extent of the injury is prognostically significant. *Frostbit* starts at the acra. First-degree frostbite leads to vasoconstriction sometimes to the point of ischemia. Brief and fairly superficial exposur to cold results in erythema and paresthesia followed by complete recovery. Longer and deeper exposure leads to blister formation (second-degree frostbite) or necrosis (third-degree frostbite).

Chemical burns due to alkalis and certain acids are of special impor tance in the field of occupational dermatoses. Chromic acid cause circumscribed ulceration of the skin. Arsenical compounds ma produce eczema and ulceration. Bleaching of hair with undilated per oxide solution frequently results in damage to the scalp. Indiscrimi nate use of phenol as a disinfectant or caustic agent also may caus considerable damage.

In addition to accidental injuries, skin damage is sometimes produced deliberately by certain patients with the aid of chemical agents A popular and easily available agent for the production of suc *artefacts* is glacial acetic acid (50 to 80 per cent acetic acid) (Figs. 21 and 212).

Electrical injuries of the skin may be produced with any electrical device having a voltage of 60 V or more. Depending on the condition of the exposure, localized or extensive burns may result.

Ionizing radiation (X-rays, grenz rays, radium, radiocobalt, thorium X may produce varying degrees of *radiodermatitis*, depending on th dosage administered; the latent period may range from 1 to 12 days

Acute radiodermatitis: First degree radiodermatitis is characterized b erythema and edema, followed by patchy hyperpigmentation, temporar alopecia, and transient reduction of sebum production. A second degree injury produces erythema, edema, vesiculation (Fig. 213 irreversible loss of nails and hair, and diminished sebaceous glan activity. Third-degree radiodermatitis leads to acute roentgen ulcer i addition to the skin changes described above.

hronic radiodermatitis can be caused by repeated small exposures or ingle large doses of ionizing radiation that initially were followed by irst- to third-degree acute radiodermatitis. Atrophy, telangiectasia, epigmentation or hyperpigmentation, permanent alopecia, shedding of nails, and keratotic changes are seen after varying periods of time. ate complications of chronic radiodermatitis are *chronic radiation ulcer* (Figs. 214 and 215) and *X-ray cancer* (both basal cell epithelioma nd prickle cell carcinoma). These may occur as late as 10 to 20 years fter the original damage.

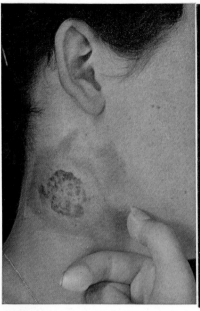

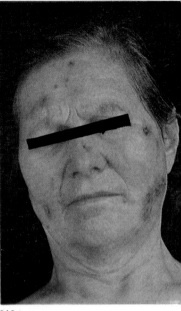

211

212

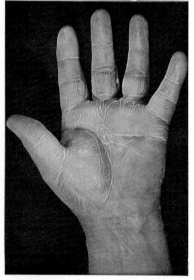

211 Factitial ulcer. Chemical burn due to acetic acid. Erythema and superficial ulceration of the neck; bullae of thumb and index finger.

212 Neurotic excoriations. Patient had delusions of parasitosis.

213 Acute radiodermatitis. Severe bullous reaction following shortly after excessive dosage of X-rays.

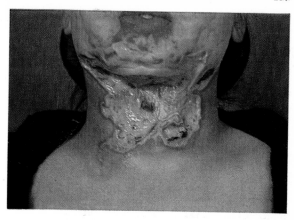

214 X-ray ulcer. Following excessive dosage of X-rays for hypertrichosis.

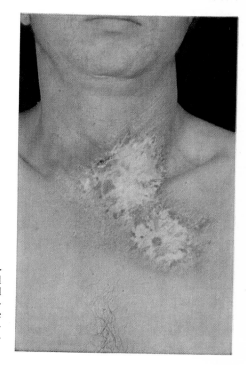

215 Chronic radioderma-titis. White sclerotic and atrophic areas with marked telangiectasia and small ulcerations due to overdosage of X-rays in a diagnostic attempt to localize metal particles.

Leukemias and Lymphomas

Uncontrolled proliferation of the cells of the hemopoietic system may lead to appearance of pathological cells in the peripheral blood and occasionally, in the skin. More frequently, however, the pathological process originates in and remains confined to the skin. Proliferation of immature forms of white blood cells produces myeloid or lymphoid leukemia; that of immature red blood cells, erythroblastoses; and that of cells of the reticuloendothelial system, reticuloses.

While many European textbooks classify both mycosis fungoides and Hodgkin's disease as systemic granulomatoses, most American authors regard mycosis fungoides as a lymphoma. *Mycosis fungoides* originates in the skin, and usually remains confined to the integument for a long period of time. *Hodgkin's disease* rarely manifests itself with specific infiltrates of the skin, and even less often originates in the skin. Both diseases are severe systemic disorders, histologically characterized predominantly by chronic granulomatous inflammation with more or less marked proliferation of reticulohistiocytic elements.

Leukemia Cutis

Chronic Myeloid Leukemia

Cutaneous manifestations of myeloid leukemia are extremely rare, while those of lymphatic leukemia are seen somewhat more frequently. Papular eruptions, purpura, hemorrhagic nodules of the mucous membranes, solitary ulcerating skin tumors, priapism, and splenomegaly are all signs suggestive of chronic myeloid leukemia.

Chronic Lymphatic Leukemia

This condition may be characterized by persistent pruritus, polymorphous erythematous eruptions, bullae, vegetating lesions, bluish red painless nodules or tumors located on prominent areas of the face (leonine facies) (Figs. 216 and 217), with virtually no tendency to regression, but a strong tendency to ulcerative degeneration. Diagnosis is made by histologic examination of the skin lesions, bone marrow smear, and peripheral blood count.

Reticulosis Cutis

This disease originates in the skin, manifesting a disturbance of the ubiquitous, plurifunctional, and polyvalent reticuloendothelial system. The histologically *monomorphous type* (Fig. 218) produces large nodular, plate-like, or small papular or nodular exanthematous or erythrodermic skin lesions. Monocytoid cells may appear in the peripheral blood. The most common *polymorphous reticulosis* is urticaria pigmentosa.

Urticaria pigmentosa (mastocytoma) was first described by *Nettleship*. This mast cell reticulosis of the skin may appear in infancy, puberty, or at a later age. Round or oval, light-to-dark-brown maculopapular lesions measuring 1 to 25 mm. in diameter are seen, especially on the trunk and the proximal portions of the extremities (Fig. 219). Friction produces a wheal confined to the site of mechanical irritation — a significant diagnostic sign. Occasionally, this may lead to bulla formation (*bullous urticaria pigmentosa*) Fig. 220) Large nodular forms of mast cell reticulosis have been observed also.

The disease shows a tendency toward slow spontaneous regression. Rarely, it may lead to fatal *mast cell leukemia.*

Lymphadenosis Benigna Cutis (Bäfverstedt)
(Lymphocytoma)

This secondary, reversible reticulosis of the skin is believed to be caused by an infectious agent. The preferred site of the large nodular lymphocytoma is the ear lobe (Fig. 221).

Granuloma Faciale Eosinophilicum (Wigley)

Preferred areas of this entity, which is not related to eosinophilic granuloma of bone, are the cheeks, temples, and nose. The lesions are sharply defined, soft round or polycyclic, with a more or less irregular surface, and of red, bluish-red, or yellowish-brown color (Fig. 222). The etiology of the disorder is unknown.

Mycosis Fungoides (d'Alibert-Bazin)

The cause of mycosis fungoides is unknown. Death may occur within six months; many patients survive 5 to 20 years, however. The disease usually has its onset in the second half of life and may manifest itself in three different forms: the *classic progressive type* (d'Alibert-Bazin), the *erythrodermic type* (Hallopeau-Besnier, "l'homme rouge"), and the *"d'emblée"* type (Vidal-Brocq), which begins with tumors.

The *initial stage* of *classic mycosis fungoides* is characterized by nonspecific, pruritic, evanescent urticarial patches, eczematous lesions, psoriasiform or parapsoriatic eruptions, and — occasionally — vesicular changes (erythematous, premycotic or prefungoid stage).

The *second stage* shows flat and nodular infiltrations (plaque stage) (Figs. 223 and 224); the *third*, typical mycotic tumors (tumor stage) (Fig. 225).

In the *"d'emblée" type*, mycotic tumors arise from normal skin or mucous membranes, without visible preceding skin changes.

The *erythrodermic type* is a generalized exfoliative dermatitis associated with general lymphadenopathy.

Hodgkin's Disease (Lymphogranulomatosis)

Various cutaneous changes may occur in Hodgkin's disease. An important symptom, and sometimes one of the earliest, is pruritus. Excoriations, hyperpigmentation, urticarial or papular changes and pruriginous nodules ("prurigo lymphadénique" Dubreuilh) are some of the nonspecific skin manifestations. Specific changes are plate-like infiltrates and necrotizing brownish-red nodules originating in the skin; infiltrations extending into the skin in contiguity with lymph nodes (Fig. 226); acquired ichthyosis; and the large purplish, rapidly ulcerating tumors characteristic of that form of malignant lymphogranulomatosis that originates primarily in the skin.

Systemic symptoms of Hodgkin's disease are unilateral cervical lymphadenopathy, intermittent fever (Pel-Ebstein type), anemia, eosinophilia, intolerance to alcohol, and progressive involvement of lymph nodes.

216 Chronic lymphatic leukemia. Reddish-blue, painless, tumorous infiltrates of the eyebrow region.

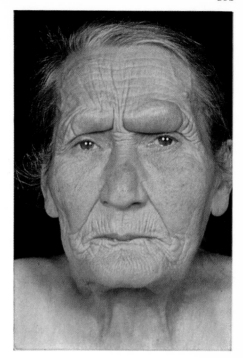

217 Chronic lymphatic leukemia. Disseminated papular infiltrates of the back and extremities with marked pruritus.

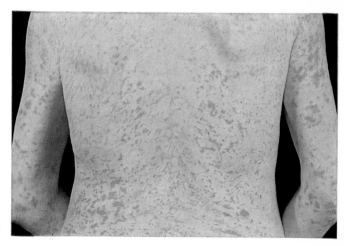

217

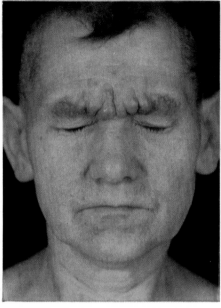

218

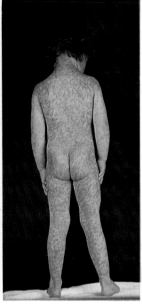

219

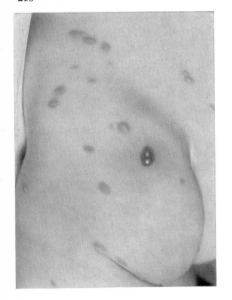

218 Reticulosis cutis. With large nodular lesions of the face (histologically mono morphous type).

219 Urticaria pigmentosa. Generalized brownish ma culopapular lesions.

220 Urticaria pigmentosa. Characteristic round to ova reddish-brown nodules an large bulla.

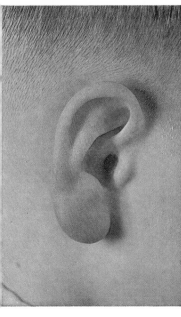

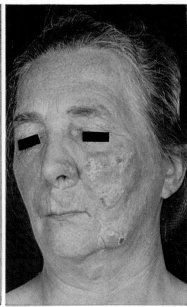

221

222

221 Lymphadenosis benigna cutis. Large, red, nodular lymphocytoma in typical localization.

222 Granuloma faciale eosinophilicum. Bluish-red, soft, scaling infiltration of the left cheeek and the nose.

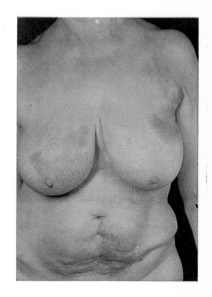

223 Mycosis fungoides, plaque stage. Circumscribed, flat, pruritic, infiltrated patches.

164

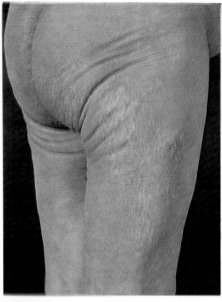

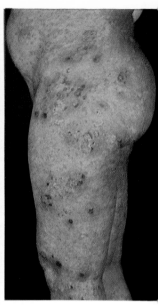

224

225

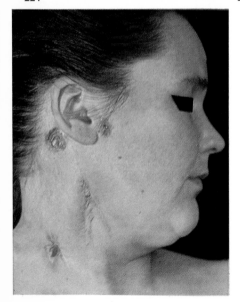

224 **Mycosis fungoides,** **stage.** Large, violaceous-red ling infiltrations of the thigh gluteal area.

225 **Mycosis fungoides,** **stage.** Numerous nodular tumorous infiltrations with ulceration.

226 **Hodgkin's disease (ly** **granulomatosis).** Specific br red necrotizing lesions inv the skin from underlying s foci.

Nevi

On the basis of clinical and practical considerations, this heading includes all circumscribed changes of the skin, whether congenital or appearing later in life, which differ from the surrounding normal skin by abnormal pigmentation or abnormal structure of the epidermis, dermis and vasculature, usually persisting unchanged throughout life. Hereditary factors are important in some instances.

Lentigo
(Nevus Spilus)

Lentigines are sharp circumscribed smooth dark brown macules, which histologically show hyperpigmentation and increased numbers of clear cells, but no nevus cells. *Juvenile lentigines* appear in childhood on all parts of the body. *Senile lentigines* (liver spots) are common in light exposed areas of elderly patients (dorsa of hands, forearms, face).

Melanocytic Nevus
(Nevus Cell Nevus)

The essential criterion of these tumors, which are also known as pigmented moles, are nevus cells arranged in groups (modified melanocytes). Melanocytic nevi represent dysontogenetic tumors (hamartomas) possessing a highly differentiated organoid structure (von Albertini). According to their shape and surface structure, the nevus cell nevi are divided into lentigo-like, papillomatous, verrucous (Fig. 227), pigmented and hairy (Fig. 228), molluscoid, and hard fibroid moles. The blue nevus of Jadassohn is rare (Fig. 15, p. 14).

Juvenile Melanoma
(Spindle Cell Nevus)

The juvenile melanoma, a very active type of compound nevus (Spitz), is seen predomimantly in the face, and almost exclusively in infants (Fig. 229). The prognosis is favorable. Malignant degeneration after puberty has been observed. Because of the presence of pleomorphic spindle cells, these rare tumors are also called spindle cell nevi.

Organic Nevi

These are congenital tumors which show an increased number of normal adnexae of the skin, e.g., sebaceous nevi (Fig. 230).

Syringoma
(Syringocystadenoma)

Syringomas develop from the epithelium of sweat glands. They usually occur on the chest, face, or upper arms of adult women as small, yellowish, soft, discrete nodules.

Vascular Nevi

The most common vascular nevus is the *nevus flammeus* (port-wine stain, capillary hemangioma) (Fig. 231). Others are *nevus araneus* (spider nevus), *nevus vasculosus* (strawberry mark), and *hemangioma cavernosum* (Fig. 232).

Occasionally, nevi flammei may be associated with other developmental disturbances. In Sturge-Weber's syndrome (encephalotrigeminal angiomatosis), a unilateral nevus flammeus of the upper and middle branches of the trigeminal nerve is associated with glaucoma, epileptic seizures, hemiplegia, and other cerebral disorders.

Klippel-Trénaunay (Parkes-Weber) Syndrome
(Osteohypertrophic Varicose Nevus)

This condition is characterized by a nevus flammeus associated with unilateral partial hypertrophy of skin and bones, and with varicose veins.

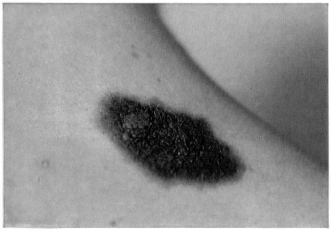

227 **Verrucous hairy pigmented nevus.**

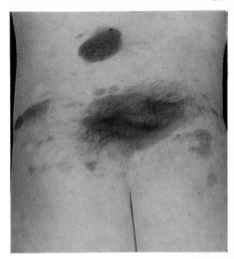

228 Pigmented hairy nevi. Some giant hairy nevi (bathing trunk nevi) show a significant tendency to malignant transformation (malignant melanoma).

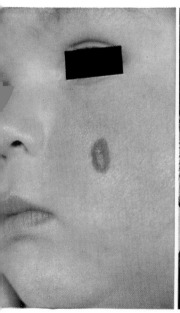

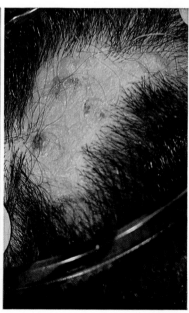

9 **Juvenile melanoma (spindle cell vus).** Reddish, raised, hairless tumor the cheek of an infant.

230 Nevus sebaceus (Jadassohn). Yellowish-red firm plaque present since birth. Basal cell epithelioma may develop in later stages.

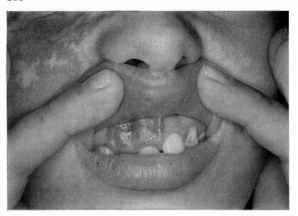

231 Nevus flammeus. Irregular, flat, reddish-blue discoloration of the right cheek and oral mucosa of the lips and gums.

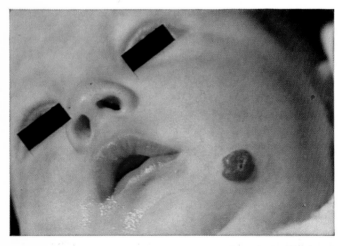

232 Nevus vasculosus (strawberry mark). Soft, raised, bluish-red tumor with irregular surface and beginning central ulceration.

Tumors

Benign Tumors

Benign epidermal tumors include *papillomas*, *actinic keratoses* (senile keratoses; occasionally associated with cornu cutaneum), *seborrheic keratoses* (seborrheic warts, verrucae seniles (Fig. 233), *keratoacanthomas* (often resembling squamous cell carcinomas), and benign tumors of the skin adnexae. The latter group includes *milia* (Fig. 234) (white spherical, pinhead-sized cysts, usually occurring in the orbital area or adjacent to scars; especially common in epidermolysis bullosa), *keratinous cysts*, *mucous cysts*, *sebaceous cysts*, *atheromas* (epidermoid or dermoid cysts), *syringomas*, *cylindromas* (Spiegler tumors; usually in the scalp region of adults). The *calcifying epithelioma of Malherbe*, a solitary tumor situated in the cutis, originates from hair matrix cells which resemble basal cells histologically. *Fibroma pendulum* (molluscum pendulum, acrochordon, skin tag) is a benign dermo-epidermal tumor. Dermal (mesenchymal) tumors include *keloid*, *fibroma durum*, and other types of fibroma.

Lipomas (hypertrophy of fatty tissue) may occur as solitary or multiple tumors. *Leiomyomas* arise from the arrector muscles of the hair or from the muscles of the blood vessels; these tumors are painful. Another mesenchymal tumor is *granuloma pyogenicum* (granuloma telangiectatum) (Fig. 235), an eruptive angioma possibly induced by an infectious agent. *Glomus tumors* are tender angioneuromas usually located on the fingers and toes.

Angiokeratoma of Mibelli presents dark red to grayish-brown small vascular papules associated with verrucous hyperkeratotic changes of the overlying epidermis. This rare dominant disorder occurs mostly in young persons, predominantly on the extensor surfaces of the fingers and toes and on the knees.

Angiokeratoma of Fordyce occurs as multiple soft red harmless vascular lesions on the scrotum.

Angiokeratoma corporis diffusum of Fabry is a rare, often fatal, familial phospholipid storage disease of smooth muscles of the skin, blood vessels, heart, and kidneys with numerous small angiomatous lesions, particularly on the lower trunk of male patients.

Malignant Tumors

Malignant epithelial tumors of the skin generally occur after the fourth decade of life. They may develop in normal or diseased skin. Disorders that sometimes precede cutaneous neoplasms are leukoplakia, xeroderma pigmentosum, senile keratosis or other chronic actinic changes, radiodermatitis, burns, changes due to chronic ingestion of arsenic or prolonged contact with tar products, lupus vulgaris, chronic ulcers, etc. The term *precancerosis* should be used with caution since many "precancerous" lesions show early, superficial cancer (carcinoma in situ) histologically.

Bowen's Disease

The usual site of this chronic, slowly progressive squamous cell epithelioma in situ is the skin of the trunk. The individual lesions may range from sharply outlined, maculopapular, round or ovoid patches to polycyclic or vegetating forms with central atrophy (Fig. 236). Association with internal cancers is not rare.

Erythroplasia of Queyrat

Circumscribed erythematous velvety patches occur on the glans penis (Fig. 237), the prepuce, the vulva, or the oral mucosa. This disorder is related to Bowen's disease.

Paget's Disease

Because of its grave prognosis, this disease should never be considered a precancerosis. It represents an intraepidermal carcinoma even in its initial stage. Inconspicuous abnormalities of the female nipple or areola, frequently treated as "eczema" for long periods of time, often represent cancerous changes originating from a mammary duct carcinoma (Fig. 238). The prognosis is the same as that of mammary carcinoma. Extra-mammary lesions may occur in the anogenital region.

Basal Cell Epithelioma
(Basal Cell Carcinoma)

These tumors (Figs. 239—243) are localized most frequently in the upper two-thirds of the face, but may also occur on the trunk (usually as multiple lesions). Their rate of growth is extremely slow. Morphologically, the cellular constituents of these neoplasms resemble basal cells. Metastatic dissemination is virtually absent, but local destruction may be considerable.

Clinical variants are the *nodulo-ulcerative* type (including rodent ulcer) (Fig. 239), the *cystic* (Fig. 243) and the *superficial* type, *morphea-like* (fibrosing), *cicatrizing* (Fig. 240) and *pigmented* basal cell epitheliomas, and the locally invasive *ulcus terebrans* type with deep ulcers and bone involvement (Figs. 241 and 242).

Squamous Cell Carcinoma
(Epidermoid Carcinoma, Prickle Cell Cancer)

This tumor combines the usual characteristics of malignancy (destructive, infiltrating growth, metastatic dissemination, general anemia, and cachexia) with a tendency to keratinization or marked dedifferentiation of its cellular elements.

These tumors have a predilection for the mucocutaneous junctions and the mucous membranes. In general, squamous cell carcinomas develop on the basis of chronically inflamed or degenerating cutaneous tissue, rather than in normal skin. Metastatic dissemination to regional lymph nodes and, at an advanced stage, to internal organs may occur. Prognosis differs for specific types of squamous cell carcinoma, such as *carcinoma of the lip, tongue,* and *external genitalia (penis* and *vulva)* (Figs. 241—251).

Secondary Metastatic Tumors of the Skin

Malignancies of internal organs rarely metastasize to the skin, whether by hematogenous or lymphogenous dissemination, or by contiguity. The histological structure of such metastatic growths usually reveals the site and structure of the primary tumor. Skin metastases arise most frequently from mammary carcinoma (Fig. 252), where lymphogenous dissemination *(lymphangiosis carcinomatosa, carcinoma erysipelatoides)* and/or dissemination by contiguity *(cancer en cuirasse)* may lead to extensive involvement (Fig. 253).

Other rare skin metastases arise from malignant melanomas, adenocarcinomas of the gastrointestinal tract (Fig. 254), bronchogenic carcinomas (Fig. 255), and hypernephromas.

Lentigo Maligna
(Melanotic Freckle of Hutchinson; Melanosis Circumscripta Praecancerosa Dubreuilh)

The preferred area of this irregularly pigmented, initially light brown, later almost black macular lesion is the upper portion of the face, but it may occur on any other exposed part of the integument. Malignant lentigo usually occurs during the latter half of life. In a high percentage of cases, it may develop into a malignant melanoma. Indurated or ulcerating nodules arising from the pigmented lesion are highly suggestive for malignant degeneration.

Malignant Melanoma

This tumor may occur at any age, but is rare before puberty, and reaches its highest incidence in the sixth decade of life.

Malignant melanoma may develop on the basis of degenerating pigmented nevi or malignant lentigo, or may arise from apparently normal skin. The clinical course of this most malignant of human tumors is unpredictable. Differential diagnosis includes all types of pigmented nevi, seborrheic keratoses, granuloma pyogenicum, and Bowen's disease. Melanomas may present as circular, kidney-shaped, or polycyclic lesions. Pigmentation may vary from brown to black. The surface of the lesion is often irregular, sometimes dome-shaped and glistening (Figs. 256 and 257). Characteristic features are considerable fragility and tendency to hemorrhage. Pinhead-sized satellite tumors are often seen surrounding the primary lesion (Figs. 258 and 259). There is an extremely great tendency to hematogenous dissemination, even at a relatively early stage. Thus, inconspicuous melanomas of the skin may have metastasized to internal organs before regional lymphadenopathy is demonstrable.

Three gross clinical forms can be defined by their morphologic and microscopic characteristics (Clark).

Lentigo maligna melanoma: This least malignant form of melanoma develops on exposed surfaces of the body of elderly patients. It starts as a relatively large, flat freckle with varied brown, tan to black coloration (Hutchinson's freckle, lentigo maligna), in which irregularly scattered black nodules evolve slowly several years after onset of the original lesion.

Superficial spreading melanoma: This lesion is often smaller than lentigo maligna melanoma. It is slightly palpable and characterized by a relatively flat central portion with an arciform indented irregular border, and shows combinations of bizarre coloring varying from brown and black to gray and pink. The malignant potential of the lesion depends on its depth of extension.

Nodular melanoma: This rapidly growing most dangerous form of melanoma is elevated throughout. Its coloration is a relatively uniform blue or black. At times, these nodules become quite large and polypoid. Usually, when nodular melanoma is first seen, it has already penetrated deeply, and death is likely in half of all patients.

Sarcomas

Sarcomas are malignant tumors of mesenchymal origin. They show infiltrating, destructive, and metastatic growth, but do not occur systemically.

Primary sarcomas of the skin originate in the integument and may occur as solitary or multiple tumors. Secondary cutaneous sarcomas spread to the integument as metastases from sarcomas of internal organs or from primary skin sarcomas. The cellular elements of sarcomas resemble embryonic round or spindle cells, reticulum cells (Fig. 260) or more highly differentiated mesenchymal tissues (e.g., fibroplastic and angioplastic sarcomas).

Dermatofibrosarcoma Protuberans

This mesenchymal tumor develops slowly over a period of several years. The bluish-red, keloid-like, firm, walnut- to fist-sized tumors are frequently found on the chest (Fig. 261) and in the abdominal region. There is no tendency to necrotic degeneration. Metastatic dissemination is very rare, but local recurrences are frequent.

Histologically and clinically, this type of tumor assumes an intermediate position between dermatofibroma and fibrosarcoma.

Multiple Idiopathic Hemorrhagic Sarcoma (Kaposi)

Primary lesions often appear in symmetrical distribution on the legs and feet, but may be seen on other parts of the integument. Pinhead- to walnut-sized, dome-shaped, purplish or brownish tumors on legs and feet, often arising from a firm edematous plaque, are the characteristic features of this disease (Fig. 262). The angiosarcomatous tumor spreads slowly and may eventually metastasize. Autochthonous new lesions in other areas occur more often than direct metastases from true sarcomatous neoplasms.

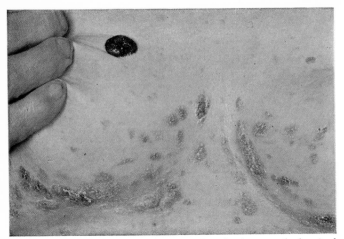

233 Seborrheic keratoses. Numerous sharply circumscribed, raised, soft, yellowish-brown, "stuck-on" tumors with irregular, greasy, scaling surface.

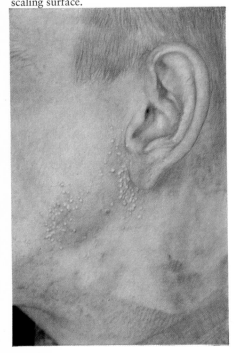

234 Milia. Multiple, round, whitish lesions secondary to trauma.

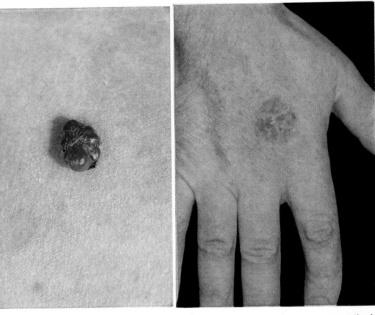

35 Granuloma pyogenicum. Easily bleeding, bright-red, soft, pedunulated tumor.

236 Bowen's disease. Circumscribed, round, reddish-brown patch with irregular scaling surface.

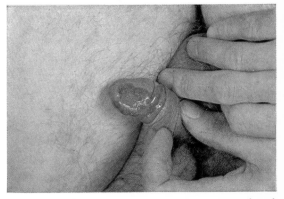

237 Erythroplasia (Queyrat). Sharply marginated, red, indolent, nonpruritic, indurated patch with velvety surface and polycyclic border.

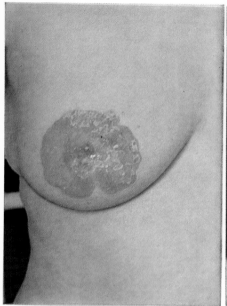

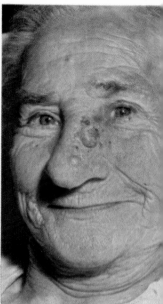

238 Paget's disease. Well defined, oozing, "eczematous," erythematous, scaling changes of the areola (mammary duct carcinoma).

239 Basal cell epithelioma, nod ulcerative type. Large, firm, glob tumor with rolled smooth waxy e and crusted central ulcer.

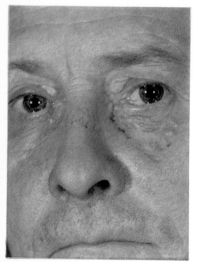

240 Basal cell epithelioma, cicatrizing type. Of the left lower lid and cheek.

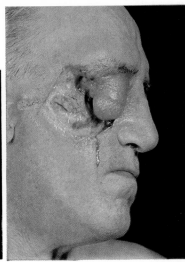

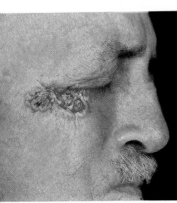

241 and 242 Basal cell epithelioma (ulcus terebrans). Locally invasive, ulcerative lesion with bone destruction. Photographs taken three years apart.

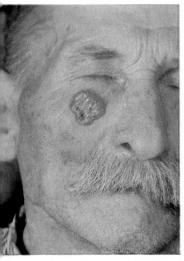

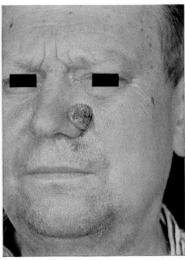

243 Basal cell epithelioma, cystic type. Large, globular, cystic and ulcerating tumor with rolled pearly border.

244 Squamous cell carcinoma. Rapidly growing, red, round, elevated, firm, ulcerated tumor.

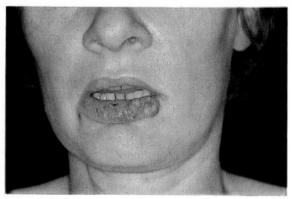

245 Squamous cell carcinoma. Large, infiltrative, firm tumor with nodular crusted surface on the lower lip.

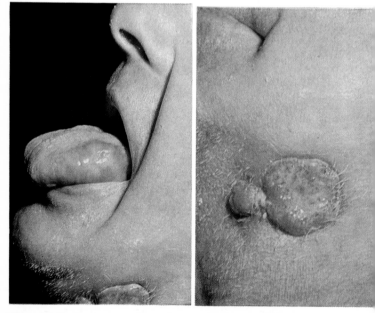

246 and **247 Squamous cell carcinoma.** Carcinoma of the tongue, originating from syphilitic glossitis with specific leukoplakia. Close-up of submandibular metastatic tumor.

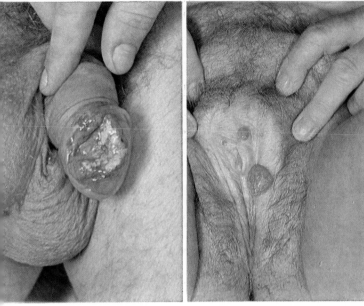

248 **Squamous cell carcinoma.**
Large, destructive, ulcerative tumor
of the glans penis.

249 **Squamous cell carcinoma.** Multiple lesions of the vulva.

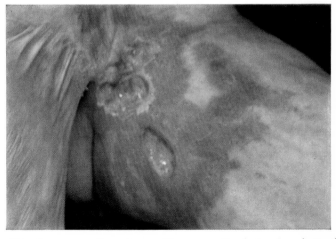

250 **Squamous cell carcinoma.** Deep, necrotic, destructive ulcers of
the thigh originating in scar tissue caused by a burn.

180

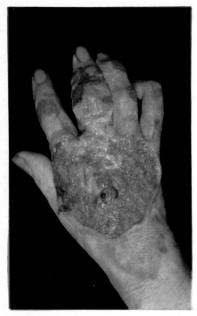

251 Squamous cell carcinoma. Extensive ulcerative tumor superimposed on lupus vulgaris lesion.

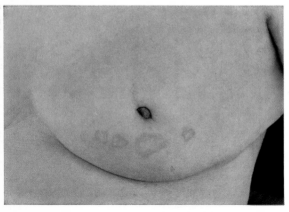

252 Mammary carcinoma. With multiple, erythematous, scaling cutaneous metastases.

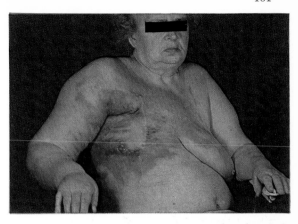

253 Mammary carcinoma. Carcinomatous lymphangiosis resembling erysipelas following mastectomy (carcinoma erysipelatoides).

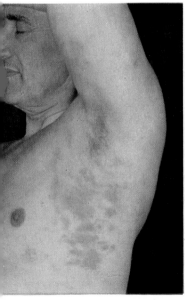

Cutaneous metastases. Gas-carcinoma.

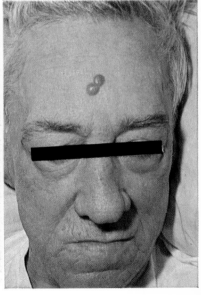

255 Cutaneous metastases. Primary tumor was a bronchogenic carcinoma.

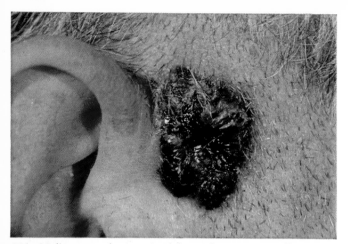

256 Malignant melanoma (nodular melanoma). Rapidly growing black tumor. Lethal in 50% of patients.

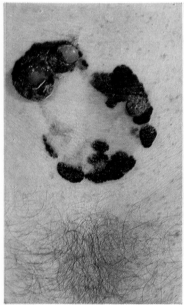

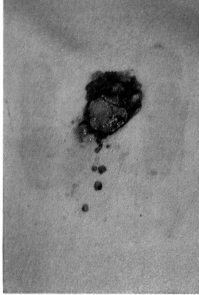

257 Lentigo maligna-melanoma. Nodular lesions developing in preexisting macular lentigo maligna of long duration.

258 Malignant melanoma. Nodular melanoma with local metastases due to lymphogenous dissemination.

183

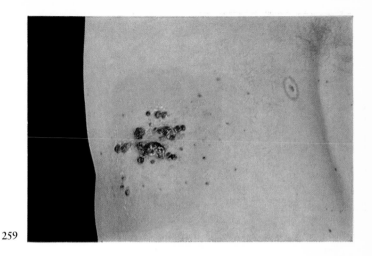

259

259 Malignant melanoma (nodular melanoma). Inconspicuous paravertebral primary tumor with multiple lymphogenous metastases into the skin of the lateral aspect of the abdomen.

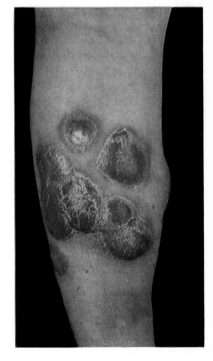

260 Malignant lymphoma, reticulum cell type. Indolent, purplish nodes of the lower leg with a tendency to ulcerative degeneration.

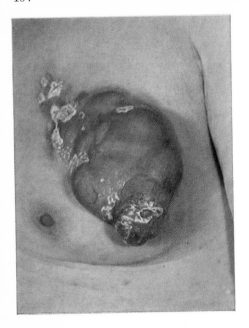

261 Dermatofibrosarcoma protuberans. Large, firm, indolent, bluish-red tumor with irregular surface on the upper chest.

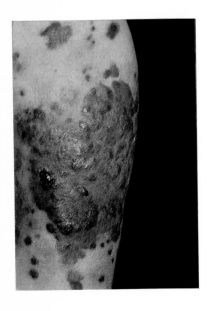

262 Multiple idiopathic hemorrhagic sarcoma (Kaposi). Coalescent and isolated, firm, angiomatous tumors of the lower leg.

Venereal Diseases

The term venereal diseases is commonly applied to infections transmitted by sexual contact, such as syphilis, chancroid, lymphogranuloma venereum, granuloma inguinale, and gonorrhea. In rare cases,
these diseases may be acquired without direct contact.

Syphilis

Syphilis is a chronic infectious disease, as are tuberculosis and leprosy.
The causative organism, Treponema pallidum, is a slender spiral
consisting of 6 to 20 (usually 8 to 12) tightly arranged coils. The
organism is actively motile, rotating around its long axis.

Treponema pallidum (Spirochaeta pallida) was discovered by Schau-
dinn in cooperation with Hoffmann (1905). Because of its poor
stainability, the parasite was named "Spirochaeta pallida". It enters
the human organism through damaged skin or mucous membranes,
unless it is introduced directly into the blood stream, as by blood
transfusions. Infection may be genital, perigenital, or extragenital.
The most common form of direct transmission is by sexual contact;
indirect transmission may occur through jointly used spoons, glasses,
lipsticks, cigarettes, etc.

Primary Syphilis

The typical cutaneous manifestation of the primary state of early
syphilis is the *chancre* (rarely in the form of multiple chancres)(Figs.
263—269). It appears 3 to 4 weeks after infection in the anogenital
region or at any other site where the treponemes have entered the body.
Usually, it is a flat, round or oblong, indurated maculo-papular lesion
of varying size. The overlying skin generally macerates and develops
into a smooth, clean erosion, which exudes a serous fluid. Untreated
primary lesions may develop superficial erosions and finally form an
indurated ulcer (ulcus durum), especially when located on the lips,
the glans, the coronal fold, or the tonsils. A single, nontender, firm,
enlarged regional lymph node occurs shortly after appearance of the
chancre.

Treponemes obtained from exudate of primary lesions may best be
demonstrated by *darkfield microscopy*; they are visualized as light,
colorless spirals. In special cases various stains, silver techniques, and
India ink preparations may be used. The darkfield technique, however,
is the quickest, simplest, and most reliable method. Darkfield examination of oral lesions is difficult because of the presence of other normally
occurring treponemes.

Secondary Syphilis

The secondary stage of early syphilis (Figs. 270—279) is reached 7 to 10 weeks after infection (seldom later), and is usually preceded by prodromal symptoms such as headaches, malaise, backaches, and slightly elevated temperature. (Rarely, secondary syphilitic eruptions may occur several years after infection, sometimes as recurrent episodes.) The lesions consist of superficial, circumscribed tissue reactions induced by predominantly perivascular accumulations of treponemes. Involvement of other organs may be overt (general lymphadenopathy, pharyngitis, nephritis, periostitis, iritis, myositis, "moth-eaten" patchy alopecia (Fig. 280) meningovascular reactions with changes in cerebrospinal fluid) or latent. Serological tests are positive in 100 per cent of patients in this stage. They first become positive within 2 to 3 weeks after the appearance of the primary lesion.

In spite of their great variability, secondary syphilic skin lesions (secondary syphilids) show certain clinical characteristics which separate them from similar eruptions. They prefer the trunk in symmetrical distribution (syphilitic roseola); the face (except in negroes) and extensor surfaces of the extremities are less frequently involved. Macular lesions of palms and soles are fairly common. Secondary lesions appear suddenly within 4 to 5 days; marked inflammatory changes are absent. Fresh macular lesions show a bright red, older ones a darker (raw ham) color. Tenderness, pruritus, vesiculation, and scaling are lacking; there is no marked elevation of body temperature. The lesions contain numerous treponemes. When the overlying skin is eroded, the lesions are highly contagious. They subside without leaving marks or scars. In exceptional cases, older regressing papular exanthemas may be scaly, micropapular exanthemas may be pruritic, or pustular eruptions may leave small scars. Annular lesions, often showing bizarre configuration and central hyperpigmentation, are more common in negroes.

The *initial macular or papular exanthema* of the secondary stage of syphilis represents the most conspicuous eruption, whereas the second and third *recurrent exanthemas*, which occasionally follow, show fewer, but larger lesions; their tendency to grouping increases with time, thus marking the transition to the late (tertiary) stage.

Latent Syphilis

The latent stage of syphilis is characterized by complete absence of symptoms except reactive serologic tests. Since the disease is continuous, no sharp line can be drawn between early latent and late latent syphilis. Most authors classify early latent syphilis as syphilis of less than 4 years' duration, and late latent syphilis as syphilis of more than 4 years' duration.

Late Syphilis

The classification of late syphilis (Figs. 281—288) includes asymptomatic and symptomatic neurosyphilis (paresis, tabes dorsalis [Figs. 285 and 286], and meningovascular neurosyphilis), cardiovascular syphilis (aortic insufficiency or aortic aneurysm) and late benign syphilis (cutaneous, osseous, and visceral gumma). The most common cutaneous forms of *late benign (tertiary) syphilis* are solitary *gummas* (often with typical punched-out ulcers), and *nodular-ulcerative (tuberoserpiginous) syphilids* (Figs. 281—284) which usually show an arciform, gyrate, polycyclic or annular pattern. These lesions are painless and non-pruritic, as were those of secondary syphilis; otherwise, they are entirely different from the lesions of early syphilis: their distribution is asymmetrical, and they develop slowly over periods of weeks or months, always leaving atrophic or cicatricial changes. They contain few treptonemes, and are virtually noncontagious. The same is true of late mucosal lesions and changes of internal organs.

The site of secondary and late syphilitic lesions of the skin and mucous membranes is often determined by chronic irritation. During the secondary stage, physiologic and pathologic excretions often induce condylomata lata in the vicinity of body orifices. Late skin manifestations of the tertiary stage occasionally occur at the site of morphine, bismuth, or mercury injections given in the past, near injuries caused by shell fragments, after repeated x-irradiation or other forms of chronic irritation.

The term *syphilis d'emblée* is applied to manifestations of the secondary stage not preceded by primary lesions, as in transfusion syphilis, congenital syphilis, or after insufficient prophylactic treatment.

However, not all cases of syphilis that appear to start with the secondary stage are cases of syphilis d'emblée; especially in women, the primary lesions may have been overlooked because of their obscure localization (vagina, cervix).

An unusual type of acquired syphilis in its early stage is *syphilis maligna*, which is characterized by ulcerative mucocutaneous lesions, severe constitutional symptoms, frequently negative serologic tests for syphilis, and absence of generalized lymphadenopathy.

Clinical diagnosis of syphilitic lesions is supported by darkfield studies and nontreponemal antigen reactions (serologic test for syphilis = STS), particulary precipitation and complement fixation tests. More specific results can be obtained with treponemal antigen tests, especially the Treponema Pallidum Immobilization (TPI) Test (Nelson) and fluorescent treponemal antibody (e.g. FTA-Abs.) tests.

Biologic false positive (BFP) serologic reactions may occur after smallpox vaccination, in malaria, infectious mononucleosis, systemic lupus erythematosus, rheumatoid arthritis and other systemic diseases.

Acquired syphilis takes a predictable course up to the beginning of the secondary stage; its later development is variable. Not every patient develops late syphilis. Only in a small percentage of all patients who remained untreated or were treated insufficiently, the skin manifestations of *late syphilis* may occur. The disease may enter a latent period without being cured. Thus a positive serologic test may be found in apparently perfectly healthy persons, e.g., during premarital examination. Others may develop late manifestations without ever having known of their disease or having been treated for it.

Congenital syphilis may be demonstrated in the fetus from the end of the fourth month of pregnancy. It is due exclusively to transmission by the syphilitic mother. There is no true primary lesion. The infection proceeds gradually via the placenta, and spreads through the entire fetal organism. Therefore, the course of this disease is different from that of postnatally acquired syphilis. Changes in internal organs take place before birth and remain noticeable postnatally. At birth, secondary lesions (roseola, papules) may be present. For periods of many years, the same eruptions as in acquired syphilis may occur, although spaced more irregularly. Not infrequently, infants with congenital syphilis are dehydrated and marasmic; the most common congenital symptoms are bullous lesions on palms and soles, syphilitic pemphigoid, rhinitis ("snuffles"), and rhagades of the perioral region. Characteristic late *stigmata* of congenital syphilis persisting throughout life are radial perioral rhagades (Fig. 287) frontal or parietal bosses, sabre shins, high palatine arch, saddle nose, Hutchinsonian teeth (Fig. 288) and mulberry molars.

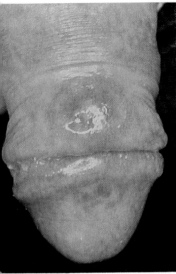

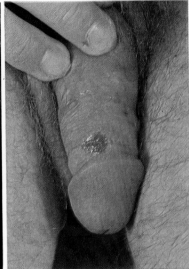

263 **Primary syphilis (chancre).** Typical early indurated clean lesion. Numerous treponemes demonstrated by darkfield microscopy. Serologic tests for syphilis (STS) were negative.

264 **Primary syphilis (chancre).** Smooth, clean, exudative, infiltrated, erosive lesion. Darkfield positive; STS negative.

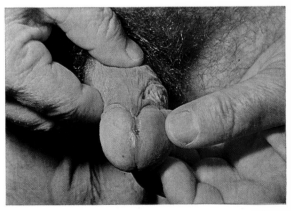

265 **Primary syphilis (chancre).** Small, firm, indolent, ulcerative lesion of the frenulum. Darkfield positive.

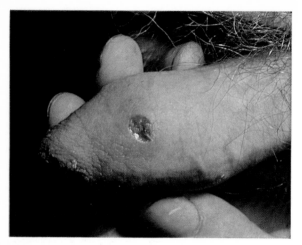

266 Primary syphilis (chancre). Indurated ulcer on the shaft of the penis. Darkfield positive; STS negative.

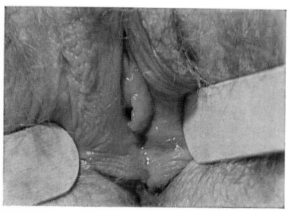

267 Primary syphilis (chancre). Flat, firm, indolent, ulcerative lesion of fourchette. Darkfield positive; STS negative.

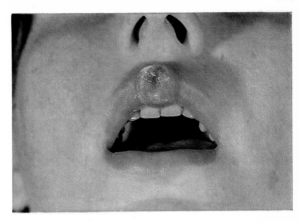

268 Primary syphilis (chancre). Large indurated lesion on the upper lip. Darkfield positive; STS negative.

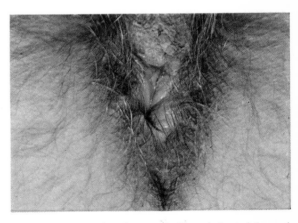

269 Primary syphilis (chancre). Indurated ulcer of the anal region, easily confused with fissures. Darkfield positive; STS negative.

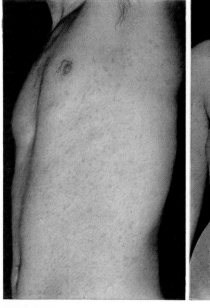

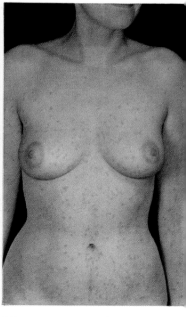

270

271

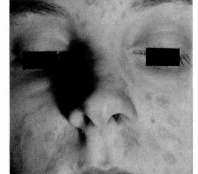

270 Secondary syphilis (syphilitic roseola). Macular exanthema with round or oval lesions which follow the lines of cleavage of the skin.

271 Secondary syphilis. Papular syphilid with sharply defined, round, raised infiltrations of "raw ham color". Individual papules are tender to pressure with a small probe (Ollendorff sign).

272 Secondary syphilis. Erythema-tosquamous syphilid of the face, simulating seborrheic dermatitis.

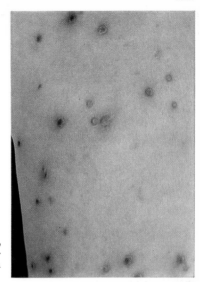

273 Secondary syphilis. Scattered, varicelliform papulopustular lesions (recurrent exanthema). A rare variety.

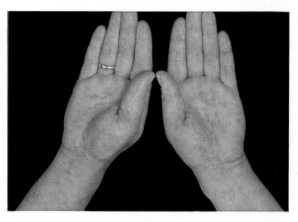

274 Secondary syphilis. Reddish-brown, slightly scaling, dry, macular and papular symmetrical lesions of the palms. Involvement of palms and soles, in combination with other symptoms is highly suggestive of secondary syphilis.

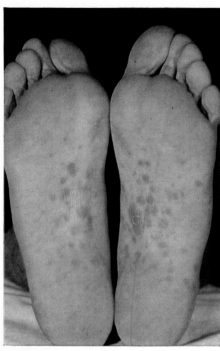

275 Secondary syphilis. Round, scaling, maculapapular lesions of the soles.

276 Secondary syphilis. Mucous patches on the glans penis and internal lamina of the prepuce.

277 Secondary syphilis. Condylomata lata of the anus.

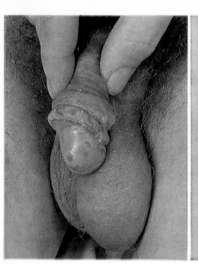

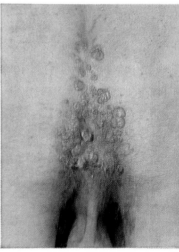

276

277

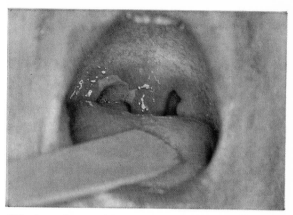

278 Secondary syphilis. Syphilitic tonsillitis with smooth papular lesions.

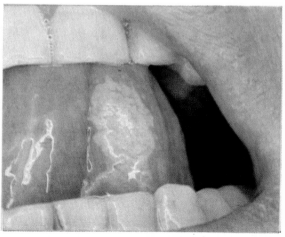

279 Secondary syphilis. Mucous patches of the underside of the tongue.

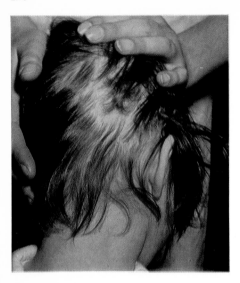

280 Secondary syphilis.
Syphilitic alopecia with typical "moth-eaten" appearance of the scalp in a 4-year-old girl with acquired syphilis.

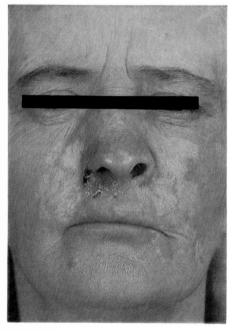

281 Late benign syphilis.
Tuberoserpiginous tertiary syphilis. Ivory-colored scars with erythematous, inflamed margins represent the healed portion of the lesion which continues to spread peripherally.

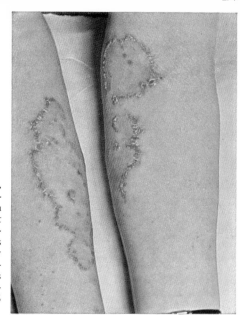

282 Late benign syphilis. Bilateral, symmetrical, nodulo-ulcerative syphilis on the forearms. Usually not found in symmetrical distribution; early manifestations of late syphilis occasionally may depart form that pattern. Serpiginous borders and scarring are characteristic of late syphilis. STS positive.

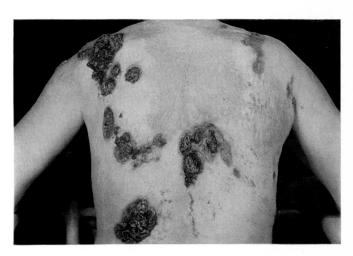

283 Late benign syphilis. Ulcerated, grouped, tuberoserpiginous syphilis wich has spread over large areas of the back, as shown by the residual hyperpigmented scars.

198

284 **Late benign syphilis.** Gumma of the tongue.

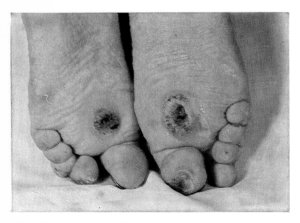

285 **Neurosyphilis.** Malum perforans in tabes dorsalis.

286 Late benign syphilis. Perforating ulcer of the hard palate. Similar ulcers may be caused by tuberculosis, carcinoma, dental fistulas, osteomyelitis, following scarlet or typhoid fever, blastomycosis, or congenital deformities.

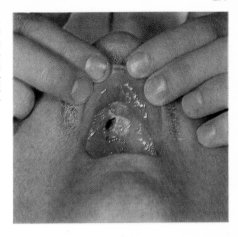

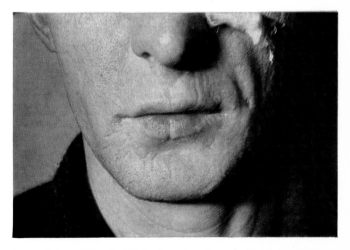

287 Congenital syphilis. Syphilitic rhagades (Parrot's lines). Radial linear scars about the mouth produced by perioral infiltrative syphilids in early life.

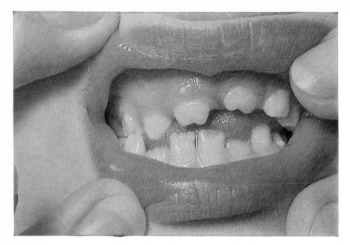

288 Congenital syphilis. Hutchinson's teeth. The upper central incisors of the second dentition show characteristic peg shape and central notching; the adjacent teeth are also deformed. Such dentition is diagnostic for congenital syphilis, especially when associated with diffuse interstitial keratitis and deafness (Hutchinson's triad).

Chancroid
(Ulcus Molle)

After an incubation period of 1 to 3 days, small, usually multiple, inflammatory erythematous tender macules, vesicles, or pustules appear; they rupture early to form soft purulent ulcers with ragged undermined borders (Fig. 289). Smears taken from the edges often show Hemophilus ducreyi (Streptobacillus Ducrey-Unna), a gram-negative rod, in typical "school of fish" arrangement. The genital lesion of chancroid, transmitted almost exclusively by sexual intercourse, is characterized by a *soft* ulcer. Occasionally, this is raised above the level of the surrounding skin. Less frequently, rapid degeneration — probably due to mixed infection — may occur, producing the clinical picture of gangrenous chancroid. Involvement of regional lymph nodes is frequently seen in the form of a unilateral bubo, which is tender (in contrast to syphilis), and may ulcerate spontaneously.

An important complication is simultaneous infection with syphilis. Repeated serologic tests for syphilis are imperative. The diagnosis of chancroid is confirmed by demonstration of the microorganismus, autoinoculation (inoculation in abdominal skin), and a skin test with Ducrey vaccine (Ito-Reenstierna test), which becomes positive after the appearance of bubos.

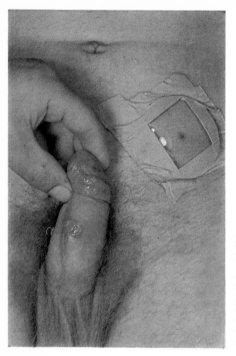

289 Chancroid (ulcus molle). Soft, tender, purulent ulcers with erythematous, ragged, undermined borders. Regional lymphadenopathy. Inoculation of tissue fragments into the abdominal wall produced a new chancroid lesion after two days.

Granuloma Inguinale
(Granuloma Venereum)

(Donovan)

This venereal disease, which occurs predominantly in negroes, is characterized by sharply circumscribed, indolent, granulating, and vegetating ulcerations on the external genitals and in the groin, usually without lymphadenopathy. The causative organism (Donovania granulomatis) is gram-negative, and may be stained with the Giemsa stain (Donovan bodies).

Lymphogranuloma Venereum
(Lymphogranuloma Inguinale)

(Durand-Nicolas-Favre)

Following an incubation period of 2 to 5 weeks, an inconspicuous evanescent vesicular or ulcerating primary lesion appears, usually on the external genitals. Two to four weeks later, male patients (predominantly negroes) develop unilateral (less frequently bilateral) inguinal lymphadenitis. Characteristically, the nodes in a chain fuse together in a large mass. Occasionally, the bubos break down and form fistulous openings. From the inguinal area, the process spreads to the intra-abdominal lymph nodes. In female patients having a primary lesion on the cervix, the process directly affects the pelvic lymph nodes. The microorganism causing lymphogranuloma venereum is a virus related to the rickettsiae, which was discovered by Miyagawa in 1935. Diagnostic aids are the complement fixation test and the intradermal Frei test.

Esthiomene (elephantiasis of the female genitals) and strictures or ulcerations of the anorectal region (Fig. 290) secondary to a primary proctitis represent advanced stages of lymphogranuloma venereum. Cancers of the rectum and adjacent areas have been reported.

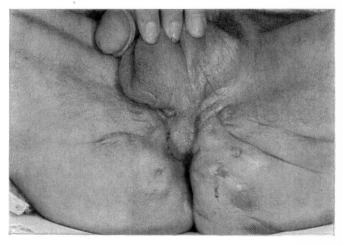

290 **Lymphogranuloma venereum.** Anorectal ulceration and scarring

Gonorrhea

Gonorrhea is still a serious venereal disease; careful diagnosis and adequate therapy are imperative.

Neisseria gonorrhoeae, a gram-negative diplococcus, was discovered by Neisser in 1879. The organism is easily demonstrated in smears stained with methylene blue. Cultures may be made in special cases (e. g., in the presence of complications of gonorrhea in women, or in order to ascertain that the disease has been cured). While the micrococci may survive and retain their infectiousness for hours in a moist environment (towels, bath sponges, etc.) infection without sexual intercourse is exceedingly rare.

After an incubation period of 1 to 8 days, a creamy, yellowish-green, purulent urethral discharge appears (Fig. 291). If this acute anterior gonorrheal urethritis is treated inadequately or not at all, it may develop into gonorrheal cavernitis, paraurethral infiltrations, posterior gonorrheal urethritis (and later urethral strictures), gonorrheal prostatitis, involvement of the seminal vesicles, funiculitis, and finally, gonorrheal epididymitis.

In the sexually mature female, the disease may involve the urethra, Skene's ducts, Bartholin's ducts, and the cervix. The squamous cell epithelium and the acidity of the vagina prevent gonorrheal vaginitis. Possible complications of gonorrhea in female patients are endometritis, salpingitis, oophoritis, and peritonitis. Infantile gonorrheal vulvovaginitis presents special therapeutic problems (Fig. 292). The vestibulum and vagina of the infant are especially vulnerable to invasion by gonococci. The urethra and cervix usually are also involved. In school-age girls, complications of ascending gonorrhea must be taken into consideration.

Extragenital gonorrheal infections are *gonoblennorrhea neonatorum* and *gonoblennorrhea adultorum* (gonorrheal conjunctivitis) (Fig. 293).

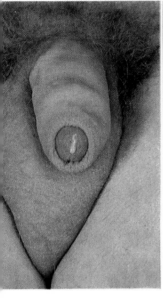 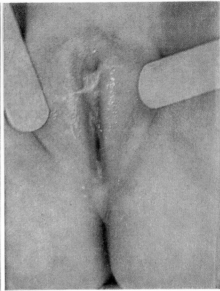

292

Gonorrheal urethritis. Crea-
purulent discharge from the
:hra.

Gonorrheal vulvovaginitis in
ncy. Edema, erythema, and
ulent discharge from the vagina,
ibulum, urethral orifice, and
a majora and minora.

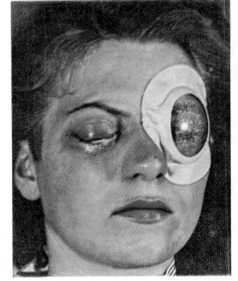

Gonorrhea of eye (gono-
norrhea). Severe inflammatory
ma of both eyelids and purulent
junctivitis due to accidental
tamination with gonorrheal

Kimmig et al., Color Atlas

Yaws

(Frambesia, Pian)

Yaws is not a venereal disease. Unlike syphilis, it is usually transmitted through direct extragenital contact. The causative organism, Treponema pertenue, resembles Treponema pallidum in appearance, motility, and stainability; it was discovered by Castellani in 1905. The close relationship between syphilis and yaws justifies discussion of the latter in this context.

Infection is extragenital in about 99 per cent of all cases; in approximately 90 per cent, this takes place during childhood. The microorganism enters the host organism through small injuries, fissures, or scratches. The primary lesions often appear on the lower extremities. The disease, which is confined to tropical and subtropical regions, starts after an incubation period of 2 to 4 weeks with a small papule or pustule; prodromal symptoms are fairly common. This *primary lesion* rapidly grows, erodes, and forms a crust (Fig. 294). Occasionally, papillomatous or ulcerative primary lesions are seen. They subside after 6 weeks, or may persist for several months.

The *secondary stage* is usually preceded by generalized lymphadenopathy. Manifestation of the secondary stage, characterized by an exanthematous eruption, may take from 3 weeks to 3 months; predilection areas are the extremities and the face. The initial exanthema consists of small papules; some regress, but the majority develop into larger papillomas with superficial granulating erosions. It is from this raspberry-like appearance of the lesions (raspberry = framboise) that the disease derives its name (Fig. 295 and 296). The lesions may coalesce, giving rise to large ulcerations. The secondary stage is characterized by frequent recurrences over periods ranging from several months to two years. A latent period follows which may either terminate the disease or mark the transition to the *tertiary or late stage*. This shows isolated lesions resembling those of tertiary syphilis, which lead to extensive tissue destruction. Severe osseous involvement may occur, resulting in deformities. *Gangosa* (rhinopharyngitis mutilans) is a special form of tertiary yaws (Fig. 297); it causes severe mutilations of nose and palate, destroying soft tissue as well as bone and cartilage. Serological tests for syphilis are positive in yaws.

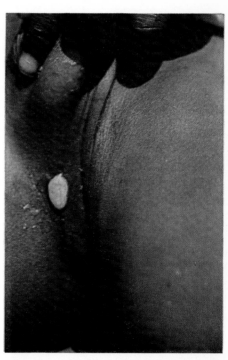

294 Yaws, primary stage. Primary lesion at the portal of entry of Treponema pertenue.

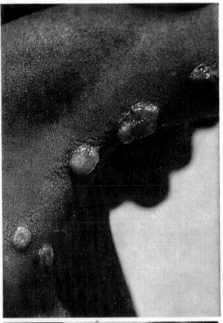

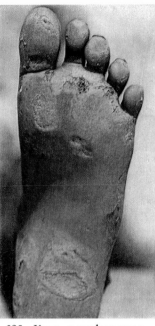

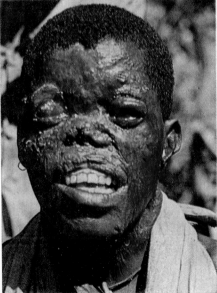

295 Yaws, secondary stage. Raspberry-like, superficially eroded, and granulomatous papillomas of the posterior axillary fold.

296 Yaws, secondary stage. Hyperkeratotic, scaling papular lesions of the sole.

297 Yaws, late stage. Gangosa (rhinopharyngitis mutilans) with severe destruction of soft tissue and bones.

Diseases of the Tongue

Enanthemas and changes of the oral mucosa associated with various dermatoses have been discussed in the respective chapters. The following remain to be mentioned:

Leukoplakia

Granulomatous inflammatory diseases (e.g., syphilis), chemical agents (tar products in cigarette smoke, arsenic), or physical irritants (galvanic and thermal) may be responsible for keratinization of the oral mucosa, which is sometimes followed by cancerous degeneration (Fig. 298).

Plummer-Vinson Syndrome

Glossitis, dysphagia, and perlèche may occur as a result of iron deficiency anemia (Fig. 299).

"Antibiotic Tongue"

During tetracycline treatment, the mucosa of the tongue often assumes a smooth, atrophic, inflamed, reddened appearance.

Black Hairy Tongue

This condition may follow antibiotic therapy. Vitamin deficiency may be an important etiologic factor. The discoloration may be black, yellowish-brown, or bluish-green (Fig. 300).

Lingua Plicata
(Furrowed Tongue; Scrotal Tongue)

This relatively frequent change of the surface of the tongue is harmless, but may invite bacterial invasion.

Geographic Tongue

Circumscribed irregular, smooth, red areas are characteristic of this disease of the mucous membrane of the tongue. Desquamation is more pronounced in the central portions of the lesions. The plaques spread toward the periphery, thus creating a rapidly changing pattern (Fig. 301).

Glossitis Rhombica Mediana (Brocq-Pautrier)

This is a benign disease, characterized by a red rhomboid plaque in the dorsal midline of the tongue (Fig. 302).

210

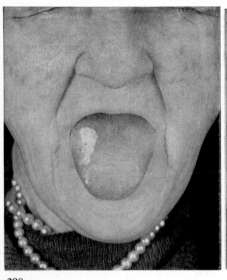

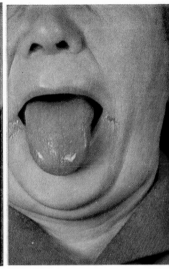

298

299

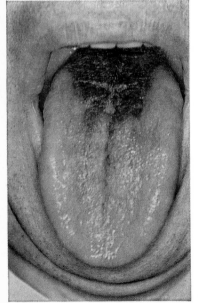

298 Leukoplakia of the tongue. Syphilitic inflammation could not be demonstrated in this case.

299 Plummer-Vinson syndrome.
Smooth, atrophic, red tongue with perlèche of corners of the mouth in an anemic patient.

300 Black hairy tongue. Of unknown origin. Hyperplastic changes of the filiform papillae.

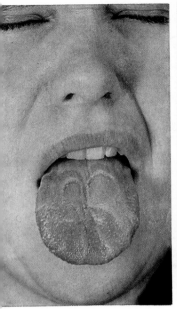

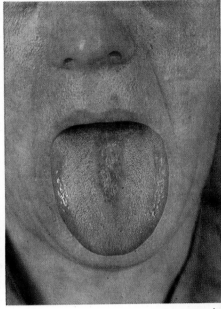

1 Geographic tongue. Irregular, circumscribed, red, desquamative lesions in central portion of the tongue.

302 Glossitis rhombica mediana. Band like, relatively large lesion without papillae in midline of the tongue.

212

References

Degos, R.: Dermatologie. Flammarion, Paris, 1970

Domonkos, A. N.: Andrews Diseases of the Skin, 6th ed., Saunders, Philadelphia, 1971

Fitzpatrick, T. B.: Dermatology in General Medicine. McGraw-Hill, New York, 1971

Gottron, H. A., W. Schönfeld: Dermatologie und Venerologie, vol. I—V. Thieme, Stuttgart, 1958—1965

Jadassohn, J.: Handbuch der Haut- und Geschlechtskrankheiten, suppl. vols., Springer, Berlin, 1959—1969

Keining, E., O. Braun-Falco: Dermatologie und Venerologie, 2nd ed. Lehmann, Munich, 1969

Kimmig, J., M. Jänner, H. Goldschmidt: Frieboes-Schönfeld Color Atlas of Dermatology. Saunders, Philadelphia, 1966

Leider, M.: Practical Pediatric Dermatology. Mosby, St. Louis, 1961

Malkinson, F. D., R. W. Pearson: The Year Book of Dermatology. Year Book Medical Publishers, Chicago (yearly)

Pillsbury, D. M., W. B. Shelley, A. M. Kligman: Dermatology. Saunders, Philadelphia, 1956

Rook, A., D. S. Wilkinson, F. J. G. Ebling: Textbook of Dermatology, Blackwell, Oxford, 1968

Savil, A., C. Warren: The Hair and Scalp, 5th ed. Williams & Wilkins, Baltimore, 1962

Index